LURE OF THE LAKES

A Taste of The Great Lakes

By George P. Wakefield

COVER ART BY ALEX COOK

First Original Edition Published in the United States of America
by George P. Wakefield, P.O. Box 158, Topping, VA 23109.

Library of Congress Number: 2001086225

ISBN: 1-880902-15-X

Manufactured in the United States of America in association with
Rappahannock Press Inc., 276 Virginia Street, Urbanna, VA 23175-0549

DEDICATION:

Mary Parsons Baldridge Wakefield

Contents

Acknowledgements

To my father, Fred W. Wakefield, for his indoctrination of his six sons to the Great Lakes by his moving from Cleveland in 1906 to Vermilion and locating his home on Lake Erie's shore; and for his many stories of racing sailboats at Rocky River and sailing to Vermilion to a virginal stream with a vast marsh and steam fish-tugs coursing the river.

As a fond Father he even called each of his sons "steamboat" when toddlers. No wonder we were "shipmen" before we could swim.

To top these endearing nautical names he told us stories of his voyages to Georgian Bay, Ontario, in 1912 on the good ship *Wing and Wing*. Such yarns of the big muskellunge that he couldn't land, Indians that couldn't smoke the *Wing's* stogies and the white granite mountains sighted forty miles in the distance; we were charmed forever and all the boys cruised to the beloved bay.

To the Trustees of the Great Lakes Historical Society, thanks for permission to select articles, pictures and sketches from the quarterly, *Inland Seas*, and its "Lure of the Lakes." These loyal marine-historians steer the organization through lake storms and are to be congratulated for the preservation and education of the lake's marine history, the great exodus that helped build the Northwest Territory.

To Alexander Burns Cook, our fine and gracious artist, for his artwork on the cover and accurate sketches spread throughout the script. Alex grew up on Lake Michigan and I on Lake Erie so we have much in common—schooners and freighters.

I could not leave out the past and current editors of *Inland Seas,* patient Janet Coe Sanborn and persistent William Donohue Ellis, who were so helpful to me. To the new editor, Nancy A.Schneider, best of luck.

To my Vermilion Captains I knew well: Dette, Clifford and Robert Parsons plus Charles Horton, all uncles. I salute them with whistle blasts; they were great sailors. Others I knew were Charles and James Gegenheimer, Linn Shaw, George Reiber, Don Lawless, Bob Trinter, Lew Stone, Brocky Young, Ed Lampe, Ott and Peter Full, Bert Mattison, Laddy and Fred Martinec, George Leidheiser and George Rathbun. Consequently, if I wanted to talk ships or fish-tugs I had plenty of talent to accompany me.

Contributions are the soul of this book and were the incentive for me to produce the *Lure*. To those who assisted me, I am most grateful and wish them well, wherever they are.

To my dear friend who suggested an index for reader assistance and who made it, Ruby Lee

Norris of Topping, Virginia, my thanks. And to the publisher and printer of the *Lure*, Fred Gaskins of the Southside Sentinel of Urbanna, Virginia, I am most grateful.

On a hot summer day in 1914, while lying on the beach of a calm lake, I saw the large passenger ship, *City of Erie*, sail by. About twenty minutes later a swish, swish washed around my little body. It was the waves of "*long ships passing*." I can still see the ship and hear the gentle swish as the waves washed the sand, as if it happened yesterday. Such are my childhood memories of our freshwater sea.

George P. Wakefield
Topping, VA 23169
6-4-2000

INTRODUCTION

This book has stories about the Great Lakes, the largest bodies of freshwater in the world. Romantic, beautiful and fascinating, the lakes are steeped in history. Their commerce has been hugely responsible for the development of one of the richest regions in the world. And the lakes provide enjoyment and pleasure to the millions of people who live along their shores.

George Patterson Wakefield, the author, has been in love with the Great Lakes and their boats and ships since the age of six. "As a boy I was always hanging around the waterfront of my hometown of Vermilion, Ohio. Starting in 1916 I sculled my six foot scow about the river absorbing everything I saw and having the fun of my life. I continued messing around with boats for the next 84 years."

Now at 90, George says he has kept a mental record of all the sights, sounds and personalities around the lakes and along the riverside. For many years--and to the delight of everyone who knows him--he has recorded his memories in a number of articles and stories in the VERMILION PHOTOJOURNAL, a weekly newspaper, and the INLAND SEAS, the quarterly journal of the Great Lakes Historical Society. This book includes those stories.

Before retiring, George worked in his family's business, the Wakefield Brass Company in Vermilion. He was a special lighting consultant in the firm for 38 years, noted for his inventiveness particularly in the design and development of luminaries for commercial use. For many years he enjoyed sailing, powerboating and cruising on Lake Erie, Lake Huron and Georgian Bay.

George now lives in Virginia near his family, also cruisers. He is a Fellow in the Illuminating Engineering Society, a Trustee Emeritus in the Great Lakes Historical Society, a former director of the Great Lakes Cruising Club and a past president of the Vermilion Area Historical Society.

As a friend of George for more than 40 years, I am honored that he has included my illustrations in this book.

Alexander Burns Cook ASMA, Curator
Inland Seas Maritime Museum, Vermilion, Ohio

NOTE:
The purchase price of this book is a direct contribution to the Great Lakes Historical Society and The Inland Seas Maritime Museum.

Hyde and Pie

Capt. Charlie Horton was one of the nicest fellows in town and that is why Mrs. Lil Gorbach told son, Dick, "You are lucky to be going sailing with Captain Horton." But what Mrs. Gorbach didn't know was that when the good captain stepped aboard his ship he became another person. (Richard Dana in his classic, *Two Years Before the Mast*, mentioned this strange transformation, similar to Dr. Jekyl and Mr. Hyde, so it is not unknown.)

Captain Charlie had another peculiar trait and that was his great fondness for blueberry pie. The season started with Dick aboard along with another Vermilion boy, Buss Darley. The food arrived and in the process of hoisting, a case hit the deck a damaging drop and out on the deck oozed a large stream of blueberries. Dick and Buss got out the broom and shovel and as Dick swept up with his ore broom and Buss shoveled the deep goo over the side the inevitable happened—the captain came down the deck!

When he saw what was happening to his favorite pies he let out a roar that swept the ship from stem to stern and turned the air to a purple glow. Never had the good ship *William A. Palmer* suffered such sonic vibrations, even in the big seas of Lake Superior!

When the season ended, Dick quit the lakes forever, but he still tells the story about Captain Hyde and his blueberry pies.

Contributed by Dick Gorbach of Vermilion, Ohio

The Welcome Ladder

Captain Dette Parsons was a fine company skipper, very strict, a hard worker and quite religious. He tried to reform some of the rough sailors with serious lectures now and then, whenever he had a good reason, I presume. He was always active and was often seen scrubbing his carpets on one of the hatch covers, which was a rugged lesson for every sailor on the ship. One independent old sailor didn't like all the "tension" aboard the *Finland* so decided to leave the ship. At the ladder he told the first mate this as he started down, "I'm glad as the devil to be gettin' off this floatin' church!"

Barely on Deck

When Roy Grant was decking with Captain Charles Horton on the *Empire City* in the twenties, he inadvertently became entertainment director as well.

It was a hot summer day on the Detroit River. Roy, like Navy sailors in the South Pacific in "condition red," slept in the raw. Suddenly the danger signal started hooting its frightening five short blasts. Roy jumped out of his bunk and charged on deck.....just as the passenger ship *Noronic* passed by close abeam!

Amid wild applause by one some hundred passengers on the lucky side of the *Noronic*, who had not only witnessed a speedboat accident, but had a rare sideshow, Roy vanished. The *Noronic* passengers had seen more than they had paid for.

Told to me by Roy Grant, who sailed on the Empire City with Captain C. A. Horton.

Don't Pass Me

In the forties, Bill Kane was sailing with Captain Almon Patchet on the *John Hulst*. Captain Patchet had a phobia about other boats passing him, especially if it was another Pittsburgher. They had been racing all the way down from Duluth with the *Ralph H. Watson*, and she was catching up off Colchester Light. At the SE shoal light the two ships were neck and neck about 200 feet apart with all hands on deck watching.

But the drama of the incident wasn't half as exciting as the next act, which brought the two vessels about a foot apart! They alternated in that position, one moving ahead, one shifting astern. They were locked in a water bond that tenaciously held them together. Finally, Captain D.W. McLeod of the *Watson* gave up and cut his speed and freed his ship. Captain Patchet wasn't an easy guy to beat, especially if you were a tinstacker! And the amazing part of the event was—the hulls never touched!

Contributed by Bill Kane of Vermilion, Ohio (third mate on the Hulst).

Don't Blame Me

"Red" Horton, son of Captain Horton, sailed as wheelsman with Captain W. J. "Charlie" Millikin one year on the "tinstacker" *Henry C. Frick*. His father was skipper on the same line's ship, *Empire City*. For some unexplainable reason the *Frick* grounded on the channel bank near Amherstburg and stayed there until released the next day.

In the interim, down the river comes the *Empire City* with Captain Horton on the bridge surveying the plight of the *Frick*. His son saw his dad, ran into the pilothouse and emerged with a large megaphone. In a loud and excited voice he piped, "I didn't do it, Pop!" In no way was he going to let his old man go by thinking that his son might have been to blame for putting the *Henry C. Frick* on the mud bank at Amherstburg!

Told by Charles "Red" Horton of Tice, Florida.

Yacht, Freighter and Charcoal

We were bound to Georgian Bay on *Tobermory II* in 1924 and docked at the old waterworks in Port Huron overnight. Just below us lay a burned out hull of a large boat and I crawled aboard to inspect. She was totally charred inside and when I spotted the remains of a colorful tile floor I realized she had once been a magnificent yacht. It was a sad sight. I returned to the *Tob* and went to Georgian Bay forgetting all about the hulk.

Then, almost a half century later I read the story of the *La Belle* in the *Inland Seas*, summer of 1972, and learned my mystery ship had been Commodore Alexander Winton's exquisite yacht that burned at Marysville, Michigan. That is when I saw her. Later she was rebuilt as the freighter *Marold II* that burned at sea off Charlevoix, Michigan, in 1937 while salvaging gasoline from the wrecked tanker, *J. Oswald Boyd*.

Ah, the *La Belle*, we'll never see her likes again!

The yacht La Belle, owned by Commodore Alexander Winton of Winton auto fame, home ported in Rocky River, Ohio.

A Huron River Trip

About this time of the year we take one last trip on the boat when the warm October weather is just right. We inevitably end up in Huron as the wind always blows up from the southwest just enough to send us along shore.

If, by chance, a freighter is in port unloading we pass by for inspection and turn around at her bow to get another look. And, sure enough, we could see her spar tops over the ore piles. She was unloading ore. On turning in, her stack had the familiar orange ring for an Interlake ship. On closer viewing she turned out to be the *Dalton*. Shades of Captain Lew Stone! We had heard of the *Dalton* many years ago when Captain Stone sailed her. What permanent things these lake ships seem to be!

A couple of old landmarks in the form of buildings always catch our eye in Huron. They are the remaining vestiges of the schooner days in Huron port and are visible in the century-old pictures of the waterfront. As we turned upriver two of these structures came to light.

Then under the bridges and up the meandering river we went, past newly developed lagoons with homes on their banks. Swamp and tree laden banks, quite different from our shale bound cliffs at Vermilion, were on all sides. We were fascinated by the length and depth of the mighty Huron. No wonder they built ships six miles up!

Why not explore the Milan Canal on this trip, since it is near Fries' Landing where the schooners were built so many years ago? And so this was our goal.

Amidst tall trees and fallen boughs we found the canal on the left bank. Carefully we nosed our way to enter, but grounded at the portal. A hundred years had filled the canal solidly with silt. Our trip up the canal was a short one—three feet!

Undaunted, I took to the land and parted the barbed wire of a pasture lot to transgress the canal bottom. The cattle use it unknowingly and they leave deep cloven imprints where schooners used to tread. A hundred feet from the river the remains of the schooner, *Idaho,* built in 1863, thwart the cattle with iron spikes that protrude quite awkwardly from the pasture.

I tried my best to twist an iron but found it impossible to draw one from the hundred-year-oak. Most of the spikes were from the center-board box of the hull. The board remained intact, even to a forged pendant eye. (Someone had attacked it with an axe and hammer.) Then, looking aft about fifty feet, a few more spikes and a rudder appeared. It was hard to starboard and rotted off a foot from the ground. So here were the bones of an old sailer buried in the canal silt.

Ahead were raised banks indicating the first lock. Some timber was visible at the first lock bottom. This could have been the lock bottom or gate but was now serving well as solid ground for cattle. Across the bank lay a fallen elm. It was big enough to portray the canal's death, as it could have started as a sapling the day the schooners ceased using the waterway.

We had last viewed the canal wreck thirty-five years ago. In that span of time little change is visible. The *Idaho* and the lock are in a static state, buried for posterity. That Ohio oak was certainly a grand material to build boats out of—-all you had to do was keep it wet and it lasted for centuries.

As we backed out of the canal I looked once more at the spikes of the *Idaho*. Suddenly, she was there in reality with her spars taller than the tree tops—a real live schooner that had just pulled into the canal to lay up for the winter. My thoughts were interrupted by, "You told us you were going to take us up the canal, Captain." My reply was quite unenthusiastic, "Well, I tried."

As I turned the boat around and headed down the river I glanced back for one more look at the old schooner. She was still there in all her glory!

Captain Charles R. Hoskins

A Great Lakes commercial fisherman of extraordinary accomplishments and unusual experiences on Lake Erie passed away September 2 in Erie, Pennsylvania, at the Hamont Medical Center. He was born in Geneva, Ohio, March 17, 1892. The Captain was 88 and had just completed his life story that appeared in recent issues of *Inland Seas*. He was a member of the Great Lakes Historical Society and donated many of keepsakes to the museum. He was an avid collector of steamboat and fishing history. His life story fills a void in our record of the lives of commercial fishermen in the internal combustion period on the lakes.

Captain Hoskins started fishing along the beach at Geneva-on-the-Lake with his father in 1900, so as a small lad of eight years he began his life's work and practically had become a commercial fisherman at a very early age. He did try to escape from this environment in 1909 when he ran away from home and shipped out on the *F. B. Squire* of the Jenkins Line, as a porter at $28 per month. He soon became second cook at $36. In 1913, after sailing on the *Joseph Sellwood*; the *Onoko*, the first iron-plated bulk freighter; the *Frank Rockefeller*, now a museum in Superior, Wisconsin; the *James C. Wallace* and the *Verona*, an Interlake ship, he temporarily retired from steamboatin'.

His income from sailing on freighters allowed him to go into partnership with his brother with the 36-foot flatbottom *Redwing*. They fished in the spring and fall off the beach and took passengers for "joy rides" in this early powerboat with a "disappearing propeller." In the fall of 1915-17 he was bos'nmate on the *W. G. Pollock* at $70 per month. This was his last "trick" on Great Lake freighters, for his savings enabled him to become a serious commercial fisherman. He bought out his brother and lengthened the *Redwing* to 42 feet, installed a heavy duty Clay engine made in Cleveland, decked her over, put on a *Crosely* net puller made in Erie and built a house on the good ship. She was then a small, practical, all weather fisherman. He named her after his future wife, *Mavret W*. Fishing was so profitable that he built a new boat, the *Mavret H.*, a 55-footer, in Ashtabula, and with her he became one of the major producers on the south shore. He held this title for the rest of his fishing days. In 1924 he pioneered the diesel engine, a Kahlenberg made in Two Rivers, Wisconsin. These early diesels required blow torch heating on each cylinder head to start. In 1927 the captain built his first steel tug, the 64-foot *Mavret H. II*, at the Great Lakes Shipyard in Ashtabula.

In 1942 the Coast Guard purchased this boat and converted her to a fire tug for the protection of the harbor of Cleveland during World War II. He served in the Coast Guard during that emergency for three and one-half years and was discharged with honor and high recommendation for his service as a firefighter. In 1946 the Captain again built a new 65-footer, the *Charles R.*, at the Stadium Yacht Basin in Cleveland, and fished her until retirement in 1960.

Captain Hoskins was an outstanding commercial fisherman due to his inherent ambition, his good judgment and ability to plan ahead, not to mention his courage and bravery to punch on in spite of gale winds, high seas, ice, fog and discouragement. He was a seaman with faith in people, ideas and God. His life story in *Inland Seas* is his contribution to the history of commercial fishing on the Great Lakes and a memorial to a gentleman spawned in Lake Erie's spume. We will miss him.

Geo. P. Wakefield

Caught in a Southwester

I believe it was in the fall of 1921 with the wooden *Mavret H.*, a year before we put in the diesel engine. We had twin screw gasoline Peerless engines in then. There were a lot of upper lake tugs here for the fall herring fishing. This morning the wind was southwest blowing quite hard, the barometer was low and falling fast. We left Erie on our trip to the nets. We were fishing canned nets then in what we call the deep water below Erie about 16 or 18 miles and we were off northeast Pennsylvania. I had one hour and fifty minutes to run to the nets. Only a few tugs left Erie that morning to lift nets and most turned back due to the heavy weather. We were able to pull over six boxes of bull nets, as they were known. These were about 18 feet deep used for herring fishing at that time.

The wind was increasing all the time and as soon as we finished pulling we started back to Erie. We did not reset the nets due to weather. As I said, we had one hour and fifty minutes to run to the nets. Well, it took us seven hours to get back to Erie against a 70-to-80-mile wind all day. We had 2200 pounds of herring. The Erie paper was out then and said the *Mavret H.* and crew were lost, as I. H. Kolbe, who was the head of the Kolbe Fish Company, had telephoned all over the lake, even to the Long Point light keeper in Canada, trying to find out if we were in shelter across the lake. Thank the Lord we came through it all safely.

These were very large seas that seemed as large as a house, long heavy breakers. If one had broken on us we would have been gone, tug and all, but somehow someone was keeping this from happening. They either broke before us or just after they passed. Also, the water from the spray and seas was hitting the tug so much that it came in the pilothouse windows. I was soaking wet and the water dripped down on the pilothouse floor soaking the gasoline engines. I expected to stop anytime, but somehow they kept plugging away. I had a large 1 1/2" bilge pump off the engine running all the way home to keep the water out of the bilge. Heavy weather is hard on wooden tugs, the seams, etc. We finally arrived in Erie and found out that other tugs did not reach their nets. We were the only tug out that got their nets that windy day. That same day one steam tug, the *George Edwards* owned by the Reiger Werner Co. in Lorain,

The Marvet H., built of wood, was a typical hard working, gas powered gillnetter of the '20s.

was fishing. He went out but instead of coming back to Erie he put into Dunkirk, New York. Big seas had stove in his after cabin. One gasoline tug at Dunkirk lost several men in the gale. Some tugs could not come up Erie Bay due to the big seas there. That was the only place we shifted something on deck, so you can see it was blowing.

Told by Captain Charles R. Hoskins.

SAWS

With all the ship watching going around on the Great Lakes, perhaps we fans should get organized. How about a new group called the Ship Admiring and Watching Society, led by such ardent experts as Ms. Joy Robers and John C. Schu? There must be many others outside of the Great Lakes Historical Society who might join up and assist SAWS in reporting via letter or e-mail to this column of their recent finding or observations while on watch. It could be a loosely knit organization minus pressure-group goals, purely for the fun of watching ships on the lakes and rivers and informing non-watchers. What do you think?

Just A Sinkin'

In the late thirties there were some of the old wooden steam tugs kicking around. The McIntyre brothers were still fishing the old *Helga* in the bay and Zip Johnson had the *Southern Cross*. The McIntyre boys, Floyd and Henry, were pretty well liked, but Floyd usually did the thinking for both of them.

One day in the late fall, they were running across Long Point Bay, going up the lake for some fall fishing, with Zip's *Southern Cross* a few hundred yards behind them. It was a clear, calm day and with a two-hour run ahead of them before they rounded the point and a companion boat not too far astern, Floyd thought it might be a good time to get a little shuteye.

When he turned the wheel over to Henry, Floyd gave him the most careful instructions, telling him not to alter course or speed. Then he crawled up in the bunk and was soon sawing logs.

About an hour and a half later, Floyd woke up, yawned and rubbed his eyes. He was pleased to see Henry was keeping his course and speed and they weren't far off their destination. Preparing to take the wheel over, he glanced out of the rear of the wheelhouse. Zip's *Southern Cross* was not to be seen!

"What happened to the *Southern Cross*?" Floyd asked.

"Oh," Henry said in a matter of course tone, "She sank about three miles back."

Contributed by Frank Prothero of Port Stanley, Ont.

The Long Blast

In 1927 I sailed as a deckhand on the Great Lakes Steamship Company's, *Sweden*. She had been laid up for several years in the Huron River, which meant she was going to be a "work-house" all summer since she needed chipping and painting all over. One very foggy morning in Lake Superior, while soogying the foredeck of the after cabin with the whistle blasting away, the unusual happened—the whistle valve stuck, transforming the signal to a continuous wail! I didn't know what the other ships thought, but the chief engineer clambered up the ladder with a sledgehammer; he whacked the sticky valve a couple of blows, and the constant hoot stopped.

What a relief! I went back to my soogy, and the chief must have removed his ear plugs or remained deaf for the rest of his days. After that experience I appreciated the intermittence of the monotony of the whistle.

Lost On The Pike

Captain H. C. Inches could have filled a book with his yarns, for his memories were as long as his life. I loved to hear his steamboat stories. When he was about to retire from the Great Lakes Historical Society Museum in Vermilion (he was in his eighties then), he wanted to purchase a mobile home to retire in, west of town on the lake. A trip to Elkhart, Indiana, was planned so I drove him over.

All along the turnpike he recited dozens of stories about his shipboard life. It was a fascinating experience for me for there I was practically in his pilothouse, and he was the old man reminiscing, while I merely asked leading questions. I was pleased to have such an intimate review of his life aboard a Great Lakes freighter. He enjoyed it as much as I did and before we knew it we had passed our exit at Elkhart! He then fumed and fussed about overshooting our port of call—perhaps his first navigational error where his dead reckoning went awry. I think what really griped him was the fact that he had another toll to pay!

But later, the good captain enjoyed several years in his new home, watching the ships go by and dreaming of his past life on the lakes. He was a rare and unusual individual, one I will always consider as a sailor of the old school who manned wooden ships in an age obscured by reality but still perceptible in history.

The Shootin' Mate

Roy Grant sailed with Captain Horton on the *Empire City* back in the twenties and loves to tell this one: They had just arrived at the ore dock in Duluth and the old man was pooped after an all night vigil in the pilothouse, so he hit the sack. The first mate and Roy were on deck when a large snowy owl winged its way between the high docks and swooped down on top of the pilothouse. What a tempting target for a fellow with a gun! That's what the mate thought, and since he had a .45 in his cabin he soon came out with it. He had to shoot fast before the exotic prize flew off so he never thought about the tired, snoozin' old man; he let go with a blast that reverberated under and around the docks like a clap of thunder!

As the echoes simmered to a dead silence, out came the old man madder than a bos'n, "What the holy hell happened?" His loud angry voice almost peaked the echoes of the .45! The mate, now looking very depressed and holding the gun at his side, tried to explain, but the old man quickly knew what had happened. With all his oral strength he yelled, "Take that damned cannon and put it away forever! I don't want any more cannonading on this ship!" And there was no more. Incidentally, the owl flew away unscathed, but perhaps dumbfounded as to what went by so fast. The slug must have landed somewhere back in Minnesota.

Contributed by Roy Grant, Vermilion, Ohio.

One Moo to Starboard

We were on a Carib cruise on the Cunarder *Ambassador* several years ago and heard an almost impossible-to-believe yarn. I don't often tell saltwater Navy tales but this one is worth a few lines. This ensign of the Reserves told it to our party in the course of a session over cocktails. It seems he was on the bridge of a DE (Destroyer Escort ship) acting as the skipper's relay on the ship's loudspeaker system. The order was, "Bring in the bow." This new chap in the service must not have heard the message properly and wasn't about to ask for a clarification so the order went out over the ship this way, "Bring in the **cow**"! I guess I forgot to mention that the chap was a native of Kansas.

Caterwauling to Freedom

It must have been about 1880 when Big Ed Lampe sailed into Vermilion Harbor with his *White Slave*, a gill-net schooner. He was bound for Erie but ice on the lake held him up so he decided to lay over in this little fishing port.

The night was dark and still as he tied up to the dock just north of the Kishman fish house. He decided to go uptown to a saloon for a bite and a warming drink. We had seven bars in town which is a high ratio since the town was of a thousand souls.

As Big Ed left his boat he heard a terrific howling and pounding on the door of a shed at the brow of the hill. In the total blackness of the night he approached the door and feeling a hasp and pin, pulled the pin. The door opened and out flew a shape that disappeared in the darkness!

Big Ed continued to the saloon and casually remarked about the incident. One of the attendants replied, "Oh, that was Giblets. He was in the jail!"

Told to me by Dr. John R. Dickason in the Vermilion Post Office, 4-23-81.

Billy, I Presume

In the fifties there was a deserted lighthouse on Middle Island left over from the days of sailing ships when they had to tack through the Middle Passage.

One day we cruised to the island aboard the *Mirage*. Three brave "explorers" vowed to climb up the tower that was barely visible in the covering trees. The whole setting was reminiscent of a great adventure and one of the crew, Charles "Red" Horton, had the appropriate costume for the occasion—a pith helmet.

We left the boat near shore and cautiously picked our way through a jungle of high weeds and poison ivy. It was scary. Nevertheless, Bill Kane and Red followed me. On entering the door we were almost overcome by the stench of a mixture of dead animals and refuse. The animals were billy goats that had succumbed in the lighthouse! I was hesitant to go up the steps but the excitement of the moment pushed me on. I led the way and Bill and Red followed several steps behind.

At the door leading to the top room I carefully peeked in and there before me like a giant stood Billy himself, pawing the floor like a bull! That was enough for me. I let out a frightened yelp, “Let’s get out of here!” and cascaded down the steps. My fearful cry sparked the other “braves” who rushed pell mell to the boat, unmindful of the real danger — poison ivy.

In the race to safety Red’s pith helmet fell off in the melee. He was determined to retrieve it at any cost so ventured back to the house. But he didn’t have to go far, for there at the door was Big Billy, happy as a king, chewing away on Red’s nice pith helmet!

Bill and I took to the water to wash off the ivy; Red didn’t think it necessary, until the next day when he forgot all about the loss of his pith helmet. He was red all over!

Tea Kettle Days on the River

DeForest “Dusty” Holl was a boy with steam engines in his eyes. I remember talking to him in the mid-twenties when he was a real nut about steam engines, for that is all he talked about whenever I met him. Maybe I was the come-on, for I was around boats most of the time in my youth and Dusty knew it. He came by that nickname because he was the fastest runner in town. Besides, how could you not talk to a fellow with a name like DeForest?

Well, anyway, he finally located a small single-cylinder steam engine that had been used as the power for a gill net puller and he was off. He could now “see” a steamboat on the Vermilion River. It wasn’t long before he had a boat, a 55-gallon drum with a pressure tank inside, a fire-box below and a homemade stack. A “stim” pipe led back to the little engine which turned a shaft with a screw prop astern. It was a simple boiler, like a kettle on the stove, but the thing actually worked!

It was no problem getting a crew, for the kids went wild for a chance to keep the wood fire burning under the “pot.” Once in a while the fireman would throw in some old trap nets or a can of oil. The engine would take off like a race horse and a plume of black smoke brought cheers from the crew like the first ride on a merry-go-round. What fun!

Dusty died early in life and I don’t believe he ever realized that when he built his little steamer by the river it was the last one, and a definite end of an era. But if he had lived, the age of steam would not have stopped on the Vermilion River—not with Dusty Holl in town!

Georgian Memories

It was a different world back in 1948. I was seven and a second daughter in a yachting family homebased in Vermilion. Each summer was filled with many boat trips in our 32-foot Richardson cruiser, *Mirage*.

I remember it all so clearly: "Old Bear" and I, lying on the bow watching the stem cut the water; the smell of varnish on the mahogany rail, warm in the summer sun; the feel of the hard anchor wedging into my thigh, the cold, clear water below rushing by; the rocky pine-clad cliffs of Collins Inlet. The world was good.

Suddenly Old Bear, my raggedy one-eyed Teddy, who was my age, rolled and splashed into the cold water. My departed loved one had left me and I let out a scream as only a seven-year-old could! Dad at the wheel immediately sized up the situation, as fathers miraculously do, and put the engines in reverse. I recall the engines vibrating to stop the boat. I saw Old Bear astern, belly-up in the smoothing wake. We backed, and father scooped up my dear Old Bear with the dip net.
I'm 39 years old now and my world has greatly changed, but I am not sure I am any better prepared to face life's sudden departures now than back in 1948. But I remember Dad's laughing call to his teary-eyed daughter, "Bear Overboard!"

Told by Mary Wakefield Buxton, Newport News, VA.

Crash Bang

There was once a captain out of Algonac, Michigan, who was a real ladies man aboard ship and when the passengers arrived he spent much of his free time entertaining the fair sailors. He never missed a meal at the passenger's table and spun many a yarn for the admiring group.

Little did he know, one trip, that he had set himself up to perform one of the best "during dinner" stories ever to permeate the dining room of a Great Lakes freighter: One fine day old Cap was in the midst of a sumptuous meal with the gals, as usual, when the second mate, in the pilothouse, started blowing the fog signal; this alarm so upset the skipper that he jumped up and headed full blast for the deck. In his wake the food and plates crashed to the floor. This was quite a surprise for the dear ones at the table for it didn't seem to be Bristol fashion and so thought the old man, too, after he realized what had happened. He had used the tablecloth as a napkin and tucked it under his belt!

Told to me June 19, 1983, by Captain George Reiber, ex Ernest T. Weir.

Automatic Pilot and Brown Spray

Roy Grant joined a group of business friends at Put-In-Bay back in the sixties aboard Charlie Mahler's ex-gillnetter, *Sonny II*, for some sport fishing off North Bass Island. After shoving off, the fishermen rigged their tackle in the cabin aft. Now, Captain Charlie was one of those rare commercial fishermen known for their swearin', tobac chewin' and independent cussedness, traits often found among the breed of seamen who spent most of their lives fighting the elements; schooners and fish boats were their classrooms and Charlie was one of the graduates.

After rounding Gibraltar Island, Roy noticed Charlie had come aft for an audience since he was the star performer on his boat. Roy wondered just who was steering the boat and asked Charlie. His reply was, "She's on automatic pilot." With this information Roy was still curious for he had wheeled on such freighters as the *Empire City* and *Harry Coulby (Finland)*, so moved for'd to see the automatic pilot. He found a large wooden steering wheel ensconced with a line running from each side of the pilothouse to an inner tube that clutched around the center spoke of the wheel!

Well, the boys caught some nice bass and had a ball with the skipper and his tobacco spittin' brand of tales. No one, though, noticed the telltale marks of the trip until they got in the light of the dock; all the boys were covered with brown spray!

Told to me by Roy Grant of Vermilion, Ohio.

The gasoline powered Detroit crossed the Atlantic.
Photograph, Commodore John G. Robinson, Ft. Lauderdale, Fl.

Freshwater Power

The first gasoline-powered boat to cross the Atlantic was the *Detroit*, making the long run voyage in 1912. She was a 35' double ender built by the Matthews Boat Company of Port Clinton, Ohio. Her skipper was Thomas Fleming Day, the editor of *The Rudder*, a yachting magazine.

When she left New Rochelle, New York, she had aboard 1,110 gallons of gas. She arrived at Queenstown, Ireland, with 100 gallons. She used sail in favorable winds to assist. From there she proceeded to St. Petersburg, Russia, for a total run of 6,308 miles. I wonder what happened to her after that long grind with her 16 h.p. two cylinder Scripps engine?

The other record maker in gasoline-powered boats was the *Speejacks IV* from the Cleveland Yacht Club at Rocky River, Ohio. In 1921 Commodore Albert Y. Gowen sailed her around the world!

Playin' Boat

In the twenties we kids had developed a play technique that produced important consequences. It may have been unique anywhere along a waterfront for we considered ourselves pros in the degree of accomplishment and imagination. It was only play—but was it? Those were glorious years on the beach, daydreaming of boats for hours and hours. In fact, many of our parents had to call us for dinner by bellowing.

First, you had to have a ship of some sort. It didn't have to be much of a model but it had to have a small nail at the bow. Attached to this was a string about 3' long which ran to the end of a stick 3-to- 4' long. This combination provided complete maneuverability in our small harbors made from sand and stone. We could take the temper of a newcomer by the length of the string and stick, the criterion of experience. The usual area was a stone spit along the west pier which provided a sheltered bay on the south side. Here we had palm size stones and sand to build our ports of Lorain, Huron or whichever.

Artie Copeland used a freighter made of a two-by-four piece of white pine; she wasn't painted but Artie thought she was. Jonko Horton had the *Empire City* that the mate of the ship had built for him (his dad was skipper); she was a beaut but her nice lines and real color scheme didn't faze us a bit, we were not class conscious. Fritz Wakefield used a four-by-four hollowed out with a gillnet lead nailed to the bottom to keep her level; she wasn't a good carrier. Alf Buell used a two-by-six and carried her cargo on deck. I had an unusual model of a real lake schooner, the *Oakleaf*, built by Ray Crosier's father, a shipbuilder. I used her minus the spars and she was a great carrier.

But what did this all amount to, if anything? Well, all these kids grew up to be ship lovers, boaters, yachtsmen, steamboaters and marine museum characters.

Topmast Frolic

In 1874 the schooner *Melvin S. Bacon* was launched at the foot of Huron Street near the museum. She was the last big ship to be built in Vermilion, thus ending the wooden ship building span of 65 years in which 58 ships were constructed.

Jim Brooks worked on her as a carpenter and ended his later years along the same bank in the twenties, building flat-bottom row boats in George Goetz's shanty. He was in his early eighties when I chatted with him as he skillfully planed the new cypress on his latest handiwork. Jim loved wood and I would often see him rub it in a caressing manner. He was fond of reminiscing and told me the following story of a launching:

"It was a sunny day in July and the whole town was there to see the *Bacon* hit the water. She was a big ship with three tall spars over a hundred feet high. Atop each was a large copper ball that made her look pretty. Then came a clanking of mauls and she started moving sideways to the river and hit the water with a gigantic splash. She rolled towards the river, then slowly recovered and came back with the spars swinging through a long arc like a giant catapult readying itself for the final shot. And that is about what happened, for the three balls went flying a thousand feet over into the marsh across the river!"

It was a graceful and fitting celebration for the launching of the last schooner. The balls were never found, so the *Bacon* sailed without her topmast ornaments.

Snakes and Caviar at Pelee Island

At Scudder, a snug harbor on the north side of Pelee Island, Ontario, old Mr. Otter, a name I remember of a water animal, would trundle down the wooden pier in the evening. It wasn't long before I became an avid listener of local lore which centered around "kid days" in 1900. He and his pals played around the docks then, just as I did around the Vermilion River in the '20s. He told me things that were quite shocking compared to our conservative boyhood, and that is a rather mild description. But anyway, according to Mr. Otter, "We used to swim around the docks then, and one of our favorite sports was diving in and coming up under water snakes, and grabbing them by the neck! We had to be careful to keep away from their mouths for they had sharp teeth!

The kids were always hungry in those days and when a pound-netter brought in large sturgeon they would hang them on the shed and gut them. We would run home and get a large slice of bread so we could hold it to the fisherman at the opportune time and he would spread it with a thick layer of sturgeon roe. We gobbled it down with fond relish, but sometimes we would get too much of a free meal and get sick. It was pretty rich food for hungry kids but we always came back for more whenever those six-footers came in."

Eye to Eye

Some of the best yarns come from old codgers you meet by chance at the various ports around the lakes. A typical example comes to mind when we were docked at Harbor Beach, Michigan, in 1954 on a cruise around Lake Huron.

I was walking along the dockside "nostalgically," my usual manner in a strange port, when I encountered an oldtimer. We chatted about old days, schooners, wooden ships and things, all gone but not forgotten. In the course of our fascinating discourse he mentioned that his eyes were "'bout gone these days 'cause I can't read no more." Then he popped his first curiosity about me with, "How old be ye? 'bout seventy?"

I was taken aback considerably with that one for I was at the "ripe old age" of 44! We soon parted company and in his eyes I was seventy and to me he was an old sailor 'bout ninety.

Spaceage Tactics

It was aboard Dan Connelly's cruiser *Sea Gull* in a rolling sea off Stokes Bay when the unexpected happened. Dan was sitting atop his pilot stool fighting each pitching roll the good ship was reacting to, when an unusually large and quick motion tossed him from his high seat off to starboard! Sitting opposite on the settee was off-duty wheelsman, Chip Buxton, who was witnessing his first jolly ride on the Great Lakes. After a lifetime on the Chesapeake Bay, Chip found the Great Lakes great and sloppy, but the lack of salt water and tide gave him a new zest for the sweetwater. Chip's reactions were fast, possibly from his law training (?) or a natural trait, but at any rate, he saw Dan's journey through space and reached out with his big arms and tackled him in mid air!

This abnormal event, perhaps could be listed as the first time an "unexpecting" skipper fell into the grasp of an unsuspecting lawyer, on a wonderful cruise to Georgian Bay.

Introduction to Commodore Robinson

Commodore John G. Robinson is a loyal Great Lakes enthusiast, having spent most of his life in Toronto, Detroit and Cleveland with boats. while in Toronto in 1906 he won the championship of Toronto Bay, a sliver cup given by the Royal Canadian Yacht Club, the only motor boat trophy given by that club, where "motor boat" is an unaccepted word! But let the good commodore carry on:

"In 1908 I formed the Marine Construction Company and became interested in speedboats, winning the Penton Gold Cup for the Great Lakes for the speedboat championship in 1913 with *Manco III*, a "V" bottom displacement hull which defeated two hydroplanes on pure reliability. World War 1 put Marine Construction out of business and I went with Hacker Boat Company of Detroit from 1915 to 1917.

"During the war years I was with Canadian Areoplanes building Jenny trainers, and in charge of the hull construction of F5L flying boats for the U. S. Navy. After the war I went back to Detroit, introduced the Hall-Scott marine engines to the east and in 1921 moved to Cleveland as editor of Power Boating, a chance I owed to having written public relation articles to various boating papers. I was vice-president of the American Power Boating Association in 1937 but became interested in the Yachtsmen Association of America and served on the Selection Committee for the Harmsworth Trophy right through until the cup was taken out of competition."

John G. knew such greats in yachting as Chris Smith, Scott Matthews, Gar Wood, Charles Kettering, George F. Crouch, William H. Hand, John H. Wells and Morris Whittaker. He lived in the "Golden Years" of yachts and yachtsmen and loves to tell stories of these grand boats and the gentlemen who owned them. John is a charter member of the Vermilion Yacht Club, perhaps the remaining living charter member. As a small lad in the twenties I remember John G. lugging around a large Speed Graphic camera in Put-in-Bay, Sandusky, Rocky River and Vermilion regattas. And for spinning yarns about boats and their exotic owners, John G. is tops. The following "memory" is a gem.

They Called Them Launches

The first time I remember hearing the word "launch" used to describe a boat was in 1893 when an uncle of mine, who had been at the World's Fair in Chicago, told about the wonderful little boats that had been speeding around the lagoons at the Fair carrying passengers for closeup views of the wonderful buildings which were the wonder of the age. No, they weren't gondolas from the famed canals of Venice propelled by oars; they were driven by electric motors using storage batteries and were absolutely silent, not like the noisy, puffy steamboats which were called launches, and other names at times. Nor were they the fabled naphtha launches which had appeared as tenders on palatial steam yachts.

Many years afterwards I was to learn that these boats were the first examples of modern production, all fifty of them had been built by the Electric Launch Company of Bayonnes, New Jersey, a firm destined to make boating history in the small boat field before the development of their famous submarines for the U. S. Navy.

The next time launches were featured at a fair was at the Pan-American Exposition at Buffalo, New York, in 1901. Here were fifty 25-foot, neatly canopied launches, all built by one company, The Truscott Mfg. Co. of southern Michigan, but this time they were all powered with gasoline engines, really an industrial revolution. After the fair was over the boats were sold to the general public and a cousin of mine bought one and had it shipped to his home at Sault Ste. Marie, Ontario.

And so as it happens in "the affairs of man," I was invited to spend a month with my cousins at the Soo, little knowing that this trip was destined to change my whole life. Leaving my home in Toronto, I traveled by train to Sarnia where I took the Northern Navigation's liner *Huronic,* which at that time ran regularly between Sarnia and Fort William on Lake Superior. It was my first experience of an overnight trip on the upper Great Lakes and I loved it, wandering all over the ship from bow to stern and enjoying every moment until long after my usual bedtime. But I was up early the next morning for I wanted to see the St. Mary's River and the approach to the Soo.

Two of my cousins met me at the dock, which wasn't far from their home, but before we reached it they had to tell me all about their wonderful launch, which, it appeared, was the only one at the Soo and set them in a distinct bracket above the common herd.

It was early in July when I arrived at the Soo, bursting with curiosity regarding the launch, but I had to be satisfied with merely a look for only my cousin Rob had mastered the intricacies of the mysterious engine, and he had a job at the steel mill and wouldn't be free until Saturday afternoon. However, after work one day Rob conducted me to the boathouse and after I had expressed the required amount of awe I was allowed to step aboard and take a seat on one of the long side seats while Rob explained what made it run. The boat was twenty-five feet long and was powered with what was known as a single cylinder, vertical two-cycle type which, at that time, didn't mean a thing to me. It was installed well aft and had a lever which activated a reversible propeller, and there was enough room aft of the engine where the engineer could sit and, if necessary, operate a crude sort of lever connected to the steering cable to give one-man control. The main steering wheel, however was up at the forward end of the cockpit with an unobstructed view ahead.

The gasoline tank was up under the forward deck, with gravity feed through a lead pipe and a shut-off valve at the tank and also at the engine. It was explained to me that the gasoline was fed into a vaporizing valve which converted the liquid gasoline into gas, which was sucked into the cylinder and ignited by an electric spark supplied by six glass jar batteries filled with water and a compound called sal ammoniac. It was the first look I had at what I learned was make-and-break ignition—a feared and ungodly contraption. Overhead was sort of an awning supported precariously by two brass poles, one forward and one aft. The stern was of the fantail type, not meant for speed but very yacht looking.

My youngest cousin, Bid, who was about my age, did some delicate finagling and obtained the key to the boathouse—how, I'll never tell—but in the next two weeks we did learn to run that engine. We stalled it time after time in the perilous waters of the St. Mary's River, but we were never caught, and no one checked gas consumption in those days.

And this was a launch in 1902. Three years afterwards I had a launch of my own. It cost me $500 and changed my life.

A Long Chain Out

The commodore is now living, with a long chain out, in the "Fort" as he calls Fort Lauderdale, Florida, among his many memories of the Great Lakes and the thousands of photos he snapped in his eighty years "cruising" the sweetwater country. His reference to "make-and-break" ignition and the "feared as an ungodly contraption" (a note of rancor, perhaps) is surely due to his experience with the gadget. It was a sparking device on early gasoline engines that was as ingenious as it was charming, with its gyrations and clickety clicks, but it sparked an early demise with its complexities to a simpler spark plug.

So, from sal ammoniac (what's that?) to sailboards, John G. has seen many improvements in boats and engines. Here is hoping the good commodore can reach a century mark with his fond memories of the Inland Seas he loves.

The Hard Way Up

A condensed log of the steamer *Thomas F. Patton* on a trip from Ashtabula, Ohio, to Marquette, Michigan, during the winter of 1978. Capt. Jack Stevens, Master.

1st Day (January 7):
Left Ashtabula at 2224. Ice 1" thick extending 4-6 miles west.

2nd Day:
Open water to 14 miles east of Southeast Shoal where ice ran 4-6" with 100% coverage. From Southeast Shoal to Pelee Passage Light ice 6-8" with 4-foot windrows. At 0500 vessel stuck in pressure ridge 2.7 miles SE of Pelee Passage Light. *C. G. Raritan* broke down before assistance. *USS* (United States Steel Corp.) *Benjamin F. Fairless* broke *Patton* free. Off Colchester *Fairless* and *Patton* took turns breaking each other out. Ice 12" thick with 6' windrows. At 1600 *Patton* anchored below Ambassador Bridge due to heavy shifting ice and low visibility on Lake St. Clair.

3rd Day:
0825 in convoy with steamers *Reserve, C. M. White, McKee Sons, William G. Mather, Cadillac, Voorhees, Fairless* and *Fraser.* Started across Lake St. Clair at 0922. Due to rapidly shifting ice and low visibility, line of vessels ahead and astern was used to determine location and drift in channel. Some vessels caught by pressure ridges came close to leaving channel. At 1330 *Patton* stopped by ridge in 8" ice. *C. G. Mariposa* with over-heated engine stuck. At 1430 convoy halted due to heavy snow squall and zero visibility in 40-50 mile winds. *Mather* freed herself and proceeded up the lake. *C. G. Mariposa* broke loose and freed *Patton* at 1700. Tug *Mary Ann* was downbound to assist *Patton* but too late. Proceeded down to assist USS vessels. *Patton* anchored off Roberts Landing due to storm warnings on Lake Huron.

4th Day:
At anchor in river.

5th Day:
Patton under way at 1627 arriving at fuel dock at 0908. 4" ice along dock prevented closing, bow out 30-36', stern 12'. In Lake Huron fields of pancake ice with 75-80% coverage. Ran from Port Huron to Harbor Beach.

6th Day:
Inbound at Detour Light at 0223. Ice field 2' thick in river. *Patton* stopped three boat lengths in ice. After backing one boat length and moving ahead *Patton* clear. Half mile past Sweets Point loss of power due to ice in condenser stopped vessel at 0325. At 1000 *Patton* was under way again after *Ryerson* broke the *Mauthe* that then freed *Patton*. At 1225 C. G. ordered *Patton* to stop in Mud Lake. Ice conditions heavy.

7th Day:
Patton underway again at 0747. Ice in tract well broken. At 0925 vessel stopped due to *Mauthe* stuck ahead. Brash ice made slow going. *C. G. Mackinaw* freed *Mauthe*. *Patton* underway again. Stuck again at half mile past Nine Mile Pt.

8th Day:
Still stuck in ice.

9th Day:
At 1050 *Patton* freed by *Mackinaw*. Ice in condenser limited power to 50-70%. Decision made to tow *Patton*. At 1345 tow cable made fast. Towing started at 1620. First attempt with *Patton* in notch. No power used by *Patton*, method failed. Second attempt using 200-300' with *Patton* minus power failed. Cable snapped with too much power by *Mackinaw*.

10th Day:
Patton made 1.75 miles in eight hours. At 0740 vessel stuck one mile below Gros Cap. At 1040 broke out by *C.G. Naugatuck* and assisted to three miles below Parisienne Island. Stuck again due to ice in condenser and loss of power. At 1305 C. G. arrived and assisted *Patton* to Island. At 1425 vessel again stuck due to ice in condenser 1.5 miles from Whitefish Point. After one half hour condenser was cleared and *Patton* continued to Marquette without further delays.

While in Marquette on the 17-18th of January the ballast condenser was installed. With this system the *Patton* had no further trouble with ice while downbound through the St. Mary's River, the Straits of Mackinac and Lake Michigan to South Chicago.

Manila Cheroots?

In 1912 Commodore Warren Brodie of Cleveland, Ohio, gathered a hardy crew and set sail for Georgian Bay in his motor sailer *Wing and Wing*. He stopped at Vermilion to pick up his old friend of the Lakewood Yacht Club, Commodore F. W. Wakefield.

Wakefield, an inveterate cigar smoker, boarded with a large supply of his favorite smokes—Pittsburgh Stogies, Ologies and Joe Cannons—to span the weeks in the wilds of Canada where he knew there would be a dearth of tobacco products. In his supply was a box of unknown vintage a friend had presented. On the trip up he passed these around and to the consternation of the entire crew they were impossible to smoke. They would not stay lit and they tasted like barnyard fodder; consequently, they were stashed away for harder souls than the crew of the *Wing and Wing*. Maybe the city boys just weren't tough enough to smoke a sailor's tobac!

At Killarney, while tied near Jackman's store, the evening's entertainment was Brodie's Gramophone, and the novelty of the "talking machine" soon brought a group of Indians to the dock. As a friendly gesture Wakefield brought out "the" stogies. In the morning the dock was littered with partially smoked cigars!

It was the ultimate test for that brand of tobac and the crew of the *Wing and Wing* concluded that if the Indians couldn't smoke 'em, they weren't smokeable.

Buoyant Script and Bureaucracy

In the thirties my brother, Ernest, tried his skill at writing fiction and produced a yarn about local river characters—fishermen, boaters, boatbuilders and other riverbank inhabitants who were so common in those years. The story turned out to be "The Treasure of Fisherman's Reef," an interesting and convincing rendition of his imagination spurred by the tales various codgers told by the dockside. In fact, it was so realistic that the Coast Guard planted a red nun buoy out there on that "Fisherman's Reef"!

So much for the power of the pen.

The Bangers

Father's *Tobermory II* had a 40 h.p. Mianus diesel, the noisiest engine on the Great Lakes. This was the smallest and most modern marine unit made in 1922 and in horsepower and weight was just about right for the good ship. On a flat day you could hear the *Tob* coming ten miles away, and if she was going by, you would hear her for another hour. The reason for all these bang bangs, more potent than a ten gauge shotgun, was the two-stroke full diesel powerplant and the unmuffled exhaust. Father had never heard the engine running before he purchased it.

One other outstanding barker that must have awakened many along the seaway and rivers was a small Halco freighter with an unmuzzled cannon. Do you remember her? One day we were watching the ships pass under the Blue Water Bridge at Sarnia and upriver came the most unusual clanking and clatter I had ever experienced as an "exhaust specialist."

As she approached us it turned out to be the *Eugene P. Pargny,* which took the honors as the best imitation of a hammering blacksmith shop. I later heard that the old Sun-Doxford diesel had fissured the engine bed. A modern unit repowered her.

The early Ford diesels were great rumblers before their acoustics were harnessed. Henry Ford was a pioneer in bringing the diesels to the lakes with his freighters *Henry Ford II, Benson Ford* and his 223-foot yacht, *Sialia.*

But the ship I enjoyed the most in passing was a saltie I heard one night at the St. Clair Inn, where the ships pass about 600 feet off. She had a slow turning engine, downbound ghosting along on her glimmering stilts of light, wheezing and chugging as about to expire. But she passed and may have run another ten years with that sewing machine contraption.

In contrast to my many memories of diesels, Mary and I crossed Lake Erie last fall on the *Pelee Island.* As I "navigated" the ship standing directly aft of the stack, I never heard the exhaust until I looked up and saw the two "Cats" purring like a "Caddy." I was witnessing over half a century of diesel development.

And then by chance, my son-in-law, Angus Murdoch, gave me a monthly magazine for ship lovers ashore and afloat, *The Ships*. In it was the container ship *Andes* of 32,159 grt powered with a slow-turning, two-stroke 19,390 h.p.diesel! Unmuffled she surely would have out-decibled the *Tob*!

The diesel fish-tug G. W. Jackson of Port Stanley, Ont.
Photo by Frank Prothero, Port Stanley, Ont.

Yarns of Twine

In September we visited Port Stanley for the first time. I had missed it on an earlier cruise along the north shore of our rhumb line from Long Point to Pte aux Pins. My vision of the harbor indicated a small river port since the name of the stream was Kettle Creek. Was I fooled? Large lakers including the 730-footers run in and back out after unloading coal or potash.

To satisfy my abnormal curiosity of commercial fish boats I strolled down to the docks to the Jackson Fisheries and much to my surprise along came the *G. W. Jackson*, a fine specimen and a typical modern tug. As the crew piled out for home I browsed near the tug and chatted with the last man, whom I suspected was the skipper. Sure enough, it was Captain Len Fields, who let me come aboard. Being an old "steam tug and wooden ship man," I was aboard something new:

steel construction throughout, enough beam aft to stage a square dance with audience, twin diesels below emitting a familiar scent and a net puller that hadn't changed a discernible bit except in drive, which may have been hydraulic. Then to an unknown device installed along the cabin top. "What is this Cap?" I asked, for in a quick glance I was confused.

"That's our heating system, an oil burner." That sure was different from the little pot-bellied stoves I knew from the steam tugs. Then we climbed to the pilothouse: radar, depth sounder, gyro compass and steering, radio and loran. Gone are the days of guess and by God. It is somewhat surprising how oldtimers navigated via a compass and running time on the steamers of the 1860-1940 era. To locate that net buoy after setting it was a good trick with a minimum of instruments. Today it must be duck soup.

What was the lingering sense in my mind as I viewed the *Jackson*? After arriving home my musing about the boat finally blossomed. It was Ed Lampe's *Peerless*. She was twin screw, two Peerless engines built in Buffalo; her pilothouse ran to the side of the main house, forming room for bunks at the roof line. The *Jackson* and *Peerless* were sister ships in two respects but their lives were years apart—I had inspected the *Peerless* as a youngster in 1924!

A Tribute

The fishermen are a hardy breed of sailors and they have to be, to battle seas and ice on earning grounds. Their boats have to be sturdy and as comfortable as possible in heavy seas and turbulent gales. The ships they have developed are distinctive and functional, produced from trial and error in the lakes' worst conditions. They have nice lines and look fit for the task. They are typically found nowhere else but on our Great Lakes. But a small boat, no matter how well designed to calm the seas of velocity, takes a licking in miserable weather and the crew has to live and bear it—that is fishing. The hazards of the profession are real, measured in lives lost at sea—three off Pelee in '83 and three off Long Point in '84. The toll is long and sad over the years.

I recall sailing to Kingsville in a small boat, wet with spray and bailing hard, managing to fight every inch of the way as a big freighter passed close by; she was high and dry and as steady as a lighthouse. I thought to myself, Boy, that is the way to go. Steamboaters and yachtsmen may think they are great seamen, but for me I'll put the commercial fishermen at the top of the list of rugged sailors.

Hail to the Ship

From Rick Wright's "Lake Log Chips" comes a note taken from Post Cliffe that should put to shame all Ship Admiring and Watching Society members.

"The Duhamel family, who have a summer cottage on the St. Lawrence at Cape Charles, are real boat watchers. They monitor the radio and when a ship approaches they hoist up the flag of the vessel's country, its house flag, and its call letters on their 35-foot flagpole and play its national anthem over a powerful hi-fi. They have over 12O anthems on tape and flags for over 60 nations!"

What an unexpected thrill for salties entering the Inland Seas!

A Sizzler

In the summer time our family went off to a cottage on the south shore of Lake Erie for the school period, and each girl who worked for us was invited to visit for a week or two. The open countryside was a whole new experience for them and for us watching their reactions. For example, one new girl walked over to the beach to watch a beautiful sunset reflected in the lake. She admired every minute of the glorious colors until the sun finally disappeared. Then she turned and said, "But tell me somethin', doesn't the water get awfully hot?"

Contributed by Virginia Walsh, Cleveland, Ohio.

A Flipped Ship

Back in the old days, when the really big yachts were expected of the wealthy as status symbols, the Dodge brothers of Detroit, Horace and John, gave a shipbuilder an order for a new yacht that was to be the uncontested queen of the Detroit waterfront. The year was 1921 and the yacht was the *Delphine*, a beautiful steam-powered ship carrying a captain and crew of 42 men. She was not only the queen of the Detroit River, oldtimers and knowledgeable Great Lake skippers adjudged her Queen of the Great Lakes as well.

The joint ownership of the beautiful new yacht seemed a natural to everyone. After all, hadn't the two men invented the Dodge motorcar? Didn't they together own the Dodge Motor Company that built the car? Didn't they also own a towering block of stock in the Ford Motor Company? Then, why shouldn't they be partners in the ownership of a yacht as well? The arrangement looked good on paper; but, like the majority of all "partnership" yacht owner relations, it simply didn't work out! The gleaming new yacht, with a crew keeping her fiddle-fit and poised for adventure at her dock, never went anywhere beyond a Sunday afternoon cruise up and down the river. No one could understand that the owners couldn't agree on anything when it came to boating, neither about where to go or who was to be in command and who was to navigate. *Delphine* might as well have been dry-docked.

Finally, one afternoon in the bar at the old Pontchartrain Hotel, the two brothers had another of their bitter battles over which of their personal cruise choices was to be taken. Finally, Horace had an idea. He turned to his brother John and said, "Look, let's flip a coin and whoever wins can have sole ownership in the damned boat!" As their friends gathered close to watch, these two brothers flipped a coin in the bar of that historic old hotel to see who would wind up owning a million dollar yacht! Horace won, but he wasn't happy. John lost and was very happy. He bought a round of drinks for everyone at the bar.

"Why is he so happy?" one of Horace's friends asked.

"Because," Horace replied, "He knows that now that I own it he'll always be my guest and I'll have to take him wherever he wants to go!"

Contributed by Captain Jack Parker, ex Yacht Paisan, Scottsdale, Arizona.

Coal Passing

Last summer I had the pleasure of driving up to the Soo and watching the ships pass through the locks. I must say the Corps of Engineers has done a fine job of enhancing the area to assist the public in viewing the ships and locks in operation.

It was a special thrill for me to watch the *Merle M. McCurdy* lock down in the McArthur lock while the *Algowood* passed down in the Poe lock. But what a contrast in ships!--the *McCurdy* built in 1910 and a typical carrier of that period and the *Algowood* with her aft cabins, diesel power and her self-unloading boom.

As the *McCurdy* passed close by I got a sweet whiff of her coal fired boilers—a nostalgic aroma of yesteryear flashed through my mind. The rumble exhaust of the *Algowood* brought me back to reality. The *McCurdy* was my age!

A Natural Hazard

Sometime in the latter part of 1870 Fred Wakefield and his brother, Ernest, found a small rowboat tied loosely at the foot of Kentucky Street (West 38th) in Cleveland; the young lads hopped aboard and went to sea not realizing that the wind was offshore. As the breeze increased farther out they cruised until it became a deep water voyage to Canada. Fortunately for the boys, a D&C ship spotted them, took them aboard and into the city dock. Father always told us that the women aboard made the captain turn back and pick them up. But this lesson of the danger of being blown out always lingered in our minds as kids growing up on the shores of Lake Erie.

In 1940, some sixty years later than the above incident, I spotted a small speck on the horizon during a strong SW wind. Being suspicious after father's often repeated warnings, I used my binoculars on the subject. Sure enough, when the unknown became visible, the speck was an outboard boat with two aboard; one was at the engine trying to start it. They were having engine trouble in a freshening SW wind, and they were in a deadly predicament, trapped in an offshore whistler two miles from shore without power to return to the harbor!

It was a dangerous spot to be in so I called Billy Miller, who lived in the lagoons and had a nice 18-foot Lyman powerboat. Bill said he would go out, so Mary and I drove over to Bill's and took off. He raced out of the harbor and went as fast as he could in the lake chop. We approached the outboarder undetected due to the wind and the wave noise. They had given up, sitting with their backs to the wind waiting for the inevitable without hope. We yelled, and they acted like men in a stupor, but finally they realized there was hope and rescue. Once aboard our boat they recovered quickly. We put back to port slowly towing the crippled boat astern. Ray Dunham and Jack Grey owed their lives to those two kids that hooked a boat at the foot of Kentucky Street many years ago!

A Light Touch

In the 1890's wooden ships were still putting into the Vermilion River for winter layup and repair, but it was not a large operation such as shipbuilding in the period 1840 to 1880. One "home" schooner was the *Melvin S. Bacon*, an annual winter resident. She was usually assisted up or down the "crick" by one of the local steam fish-tugs, the *J. P. Deveny, Telephone* and *Favorite*, which were nice little tow tugs with their perky steam engines and open decks. Besides, the skipper got a kick out of showing off his tug's strength and the captain's skill. The fee wasn't a stipend to be ignored either.

One day in 1893 the Leidheiser tug, *J. P. Deveny*, took the *Bacon* in tow and on the way out made a "light touch." Let me record the official statement from the National Archives.

"1079. Vermilion on the outer end of the west pier, entrance to Vermilion Harbor, Lake Erie, Ohio—On April 27, 1893, the light tower on the west pier was struck by the schooner *M. S. Bacon*, while she was being towed out of the harbor by the steam tug *J. P. Deveny*. Two angle iron plates in the second section of the tower were so badly injured that new plates had to be made to replace them. Many of the joints between the outer plates were strained, the interior somewhat injured, and one corner of the beacon raised about 2 inches. The beacon was repaired and the bill for the cost was presented to the owners of the *Deveny*. They declined to pay it. The case was turned over to the Department of Justice that proper legal proceedings might be taken."

In 1894 the bill of $161.62 was collected and paid by the Leidheiser Fish Company, which must have taken a little steam out of the towing business in the Vermilion River.

Whistling in the Fog

Ron Beaupre of Port Elgin, Ontario, provided me with the photo of Captain Beaton's *Fort York* for his story about big seas on Lake Superior in the winter 1982 Edition of *Inland Seas*. He also unearthed the unusual story about the collision between the steamers *John B. Cowle* and the *Issac M. Scott* in 1909.

"Wallace Niles was off watch and asleep when his ship, the *John B. Cowle,* was struck by the *Isaac M. Scott.* He ran up on deck in his underwear, leaving behind all his worldly possessions, including Christmas presents he had hoped to take home to Wolfe Island.

Wallace went down with his sinking ship, deeper and deeper; but suddenly, he was released from the suction and shot up to the surface. He grabbed a piece of floating wreckage which enabled him to stay afloat in the icy water. Surrounded by fog, he began making a piercing whistling sound by using his fingers. A passing steamer sought out the source of this sound and Wallace was rescued!"

The steamer that located the "whistler" was probably the *Frank H. Goodyear*, which rescued some of the crew members of the *Cowle*. Fourteen members of the *Cowle* went down with the ship, and the *Scott* was lost in the big storm of 1913.

Ahoy, *Tashmoo*

In 1920 we were on a cruise up the St. Clair River aboard the *Tobermory*, a trim 45-foot Matthews-built yacht. The weekend found us tied at a dock nearby the *Tashmoo* landing at Algonac, Michigan. Commodore F. W. Robert's *Petrel* was there along with Doctor Griese's *Elaranjo*, the occasion being the centennial celebration of the town of Algonac, as I recall. It was a gala Sunday with boats all over the riverside.

With the plethora of small boats, in came the *Tashmoo* with a load of merry passengers. After unloading she was backing out to go upriver and at that very moment my father, Fred, who was watching the big ship, as all of us on the *Tob* were, spotted a small boat that had just stalled at the stern of the *Tashmoo*. What a spot to be in with a side-wheeler backing down!

We all saw the danger and quickly visualized the hazardous possibility of the big paddle wheels walking over the boat and smashing it to smithereens! Father cupped his hands around his mouth and "bellowed" in his loudest voice, "Captain, there is a small boat under your stern!" The captain immediately signaled the engineroom and the massive paddle wheels came to a sudden halt, The stalled boat was pushed away from the overhanging *Tashmoo* and another close call had been averted—thanks to devoted boat watchers!

The Fort York leaving the Iroquois Lock, ca 1958. Photograph by Ron Beaupre.

Superior Seas

In 1940 we were in Georgian Bay aboard the *Noronic* heading for Midland, Ontario, on a three- day cruise out of Cleveland, Ohio. The date is vivid in my mind because we heard on the radio that France had fallen to Hitler's forces. Another memory almost as impressive, a senior high school graduating class had boarded in the rivers; they ran all over the ship like wild animals, so sleep was a rare occasion. Coincidentally, I snapped a photo of the pilothouse from the foredeck and the officer in view was First Mate Horace L. Beaton, who later became captain of the package freighter *Fort York* of the Canadian Steamship lines, the subject of this story. I am indebted to his son, Rev. Charles P. Beaton, for allowing me to extract a portion from the captain's book, *From the Wheelhouse.*

The design of the *Fort York* and *Fort Chanbly*, with the wheelhouse and all accommodations aft, and the power and speed you could get from these ships, made them good weather ships. One trip I made across Lake Superior in the fall of 1958, the first season I was on the *Fort York*, I remember well. We left the Soo in the afternoon and proceeded across Whitefish Bay. The weather report was not good and there were a dozen ships at anchor behind Whitefish Point Light; the sea did not seem too bad, and as I had never had the *Fort York* in bad weather, I decided to keep going.

We were doing very well and running sixteen miles an hour up as far as Caribou Island. After we passed abeam of Caribou Light, the seas began to get bigger. The ship was rising and falling in the head sea. I had stretched out on the settee in the back of the wheelhouse. The seas seemed to come in threes. The ship would rise on the first and come back down, then rise further on the second and still higher on the third. We were still going full speed and doing quite well when I felt the ship rise on the first sea and back down and go higher on the second and back down, then still higher on the third and, at the top of this sea, the ship hesitated and did not to back down then went up a little higher. I came off the settee and hollered to the first mate. "Check her down."

By now, the first mate started to hang on and could not reach back to the engine chadburn to signal the engineer to check the engine. The *York* had gone over the top of the big wave and on the way down, put the bow deck right under the blue Lake Superior water. It came over the bow and down the deck and hit the afterhouse just under the wheelhouse smashing out several windows.

We kept on going right up the center of Lake Superior and put in a bad night. Our speed was reduced to six miles an hour and we were able to maintain headway at that speed. As we passed abeam of Keweenaw Peninsula, we ran into bigger seas. It was blowing about sixty-five miles per hour. I was unable to continue on course to Passage Island and had to bring the ship around more head to, to avoid rolling too heavily. We continued on this course the rest of the night and up to about ten o'clock in the morning. By now, we had passed to the west of the Rock of Ages Light and right up to the land of Minnesota state before I could turn the ship and make a course inside of Isle Royale to get to Port Arthur, Ontario. The first mate, Carl Norton, said he never saw bigger waves in all his days as a sailor. I agreed with him, as I believe it was the biggest sea I had ever encountered, sixteen to twenty feet I'd imagine, about the height of a two-story-house

To a Lake Captain

Smoking tugs, tooting whistles, gales and breakers white,
Too much current, shallow water, rocks and fog all night,
Rolling in a beam sea from Duluth to the Soo,
Punching into a Northeaster, worrying about the crew,
Gary, Buffalo, Sandusky, Conneaut, and that crooked creek!
The Flats, calm days, beautiful river sights that yachtsmen seek,
Then heavy ice, bitter weather, icy decks and twenty below,
Pushing, turning, help at last—the car ferry, then on the go,
Coal dust, wheat, ore pouring down, yelling men and a full moon,
Banging coal cars and a puffing engine trying to make room,
Stepping up or down at the locks, the highlands of Keweenaw,
Crystal waters and muddy Lake Erie, the Straits of Mackinaw,
Isle Royal, Michipicoten, Pelee, Manitoulin, and Stag,
Belle, Bo Lo, Grand, Drummond, Presque, Beaver and a snag,
Bent plates, lost anchors, missing blades, inspectors, engine trouble,
Low steam, crazy boaters, office wants you on the double.
Problems, problems, weather, weather, just a mess of strife,
To keep her steaming, hauling, floating, throughout a captain's life.

The Prize Stake

It wasn't often in the life of an individual living along the shores of Lake Erie in the twenties that a confrontation took place over a 90-foot spruce pound-net stake that had inadvertently washed up on the beach, but once it did, and here is what actually happened.

One Sunday morning my brother Bill discovered, much to his surprise and glee, a long, straight spar on the beach in front of our family home in Vermilion. About one-fourth of the monster lay at the foot of Main Street and therein was the crux of the problem. Don Lawless, a friend and classmate, had found the beauty and claimed the portion lying on public property—the road end. Bill had to use his best diplomacy to prevent Don from using his saw to dismember the slim top from its main stem. The agreement was to have the mayor, W. H. Mitchell, render a decision as to who would get the end piece lying on the road. Consequently, His Honor Mr. Mitchell, made a quick trip to the beach. His decision was that Bill should get the whole stake, since its real value was in the piece as a whole, not pieces with two owners. Case closed!

The stake, cut up to proper lengths, eventually became a derrick for hoisting Star boats in the Vermilion River. The end came when the thin part of the stake broke and dropped Charlie Decker's boat in the river! Cloudy Noel, the ferryman, who was passing by in the river at the time, often quoted this bit of local humor, "It was the first time I ever did see a falling star in the Vermilion River!"

Open Boats Preferred

When the *Jos. T. Sloat* came out in 1908 she was an open-deck gill-netter. After a year of fishing her, Otto Full, the skipper, had had enough of out-in-the-cold gill netting so decided to build a house around her deck that winter. He laid the boat up in Huron as was the custom to avoid the spring freshets in the Vermilion stream. When he brought the "new" *Sloat* back to Kishman's dock in Vermilion he was greeted by Henry Kishman, a pioneer gill-netter who had fished sailing boats and open-deckers all his life on the lake: "Well, Ott, I see you have spoiled her as a fish-tug."

Told to me by Ray Full about his Dad in 1982.
(The above story reminds me of a remark George Rathbun made when I talked to him about fishing in the old days. He fished as a deckhand on one of the open-deckers out of Vermilion in the 90s and said: "When you are pulling the net in up for'd in freezing weather with the wind biting into your face, you are sweating all over from the exertion and you don't notice the cold." Maybe that was Henry Kishman's experience, so why put a house on a fish-tug?)

A Two Blast Broadside

The loaded freighter *Leon Falk, Jr.* was up-bound at Port Huron when she answered a saltie coming through the rapids under the Blue Water Bridge with a two whistle signal. The foreigner wanted to swing to her port and go to the grain elevator on the Canadian side, which was a normal procedure.

Captain George Reiber on the*Falk* moved a bit to port to allow for the maneuver, but when the saltie slowed down and drifted under the bridge with her broadside showing, that was a ship of a different perspective. The*Falk* had no place to go!

Reiber blasted forth a five whistle danger signal and attacked with a radio message that reverberated throughout the St. Clair country like a bucko mate dressing down a tar. It worked, too, and the whole incident passed away like a ripple in the fast moving current where most of the water from Lake Superior, Lake Michigan and Lake Huron runs down hill at a five-mile clip into the lovely St. Clair River.

Told to me by Captain George Reiber, ex Leon Falk Jr.

These are not the ships in the above story; but the navigational story and location are uncannily similar. Photo by Paul Michaels through courtesy of Ron Beaupre, Port Elgin, Ont.

The End of the *Rainbow*

Captain Cliff Parsons was an independent, innovative gill-netter and was accustomed to doing what he thought was right. This inherent trait may have been a genetic leftover from his pioneering forefathers rather than having been an adaptation from his profession, which generally made a fellow a true conservative. He was undoubtedly that, all right, but he was more as you will see from the story of the *Rainbow*, a steam gill-net tug.

Let us first review his genealogy: Lt. Alexander Harrow was the skipper of the *HMS Welcome*, a supply sloop for Fort Mackinac, and sailed the lakes in the rough-and-tumble days of the 18th century. After retiring from the service in 1794 he purchased 14,400 acres a short distance north of the village of Algonac where the house still stands. His wife was an Edelleman from Kentucky who had been captured by the Indians as a young girl and sold to Captain Harrow on Harsons island; it is rumored he bought her for a keg of whiskey which was illegitimate but effective Indian money in those days. Their daughter, Mary, married Stephen Grummond of Portland, Michigan (later Marine City). Grummond ran the first general store in the area. Their children were Matilda, George, and Stephen Jr., who became the mayor of Detroit and a very successful ship owner of the Grummond line of passenger vessels and tugs. One of his tugs was the famous *Champion* used for towing schooners through the rivers. George was a colonel in the Civil War and lost his life in the Fetterman massacre of 1866.

At Marine City Ben Horton, originally from Silver Creek, New York, on Lake Erie, wooed and married Matilda Grummond. Ben was a state representative and architect-contractor. He built the first large schoolhouse in Marine City. He later moved to Detroit where the depression of that period caused him to move again; this time to Vermilion, Ohio, where he knew the lumber people, the Gilchrists. His family steamed down to the little port on the south shore of Lake Erie on Uncle Stephen's *Champion*. Ben subsequently built the town hall in 1883 which stands today as a memorial to the boy from St. Clair country. Ben and Matilda's daughter, Franc, married Burdette Parsons, the grandson of Burton Parsons, the schooner builder, and Cliff was one of the sons.

The *Rainbow* was a derelict sunk on her side at the yacht club dock. Cliff was commissioned to raise her and get her out, and he did. He pumped her dry and towed her out with his fish tug *Alma*, right out in the deep water of Lake Erie, opened the sea cock and down went the *Rainbow*. But as usual, the unexpected happened—up floated the upper works of the old ship! This was embarrassing and a navigational hazard. Cliff said the Coast Guard was pretty rough on him after the fiasco at the end of the *Rainbow*.

The Biggest Catch

We turned the corner of Pelee Island at Sheridan Point giving the pound nets a broad berth as the cruiser, *Cygnet*, scooted along the west coast of the large Canadian Island. More nets were on the port side so I kept out, knowing their danger.
"What is that boat doing in the net ahead?" I asked the mate, who was scanning our approach to the west dock.

"He must be stealing fish to fill his stringer, an easy way to catch fish," was Mary's reply. As the picture cleared I could see more detail.

"He isn't catching fish, he is working on his prop. He is caught!" We moved in closer. A few questions indicated that he had run into the net at nighttime and he and his girlfriend had spent the night caught in the trap! He asked for a knife so I handed him our lone carving blade. He cut and cut but it was an endless task. As we were about to leave I spotted a fast, small boat rounding the point. I knew it was Mr. Harris of Scudder, the owner of the net. He had been tipped off by a landsman. I took the knife and got out of there for I didn't relish being regarded as an accomplice in the confrontation I knew was coming. I still have that carving knife and the blade has a small nick, from the net. The lucky couple were spared by the gentle west winds but I'll bet they never realized it.

A Voyage by Rail

In '78 we boarded the Canadian Pacific out of Toronto to see Parry Sound and hear the resonant hum of our train crossing over the high-level bridge at the river. Here in 1912 Commodore Brody of Cleveland docked his yacht, *Wing and Wing*, while on a pioneer powerboat cruise in Georgian Bay.

In the morning we viewed the natural beauty of the north Superior shoreline and wondered how the track builders forged their way through the rock cliffs.

Then, Thunder Bay with its massive grain elevators flavored our perspective of the harvests.

Next, the great plains, the breadbasket of the world like a calm sea, expansive and gentle, bore us onward with prairie dogs gamboling like playful porpoise; then the big seas of the majestic Rockies testing our seagoing ability in the splendor of the crests; Vancouver, the husky port of the Pacific, opened our eyes to the power of the west.

We took the ferry to Victoria and had tea and crumpets at the Empress with a visit to the Marine Museum. There we inspected the *Tillicum,* the unusual ketch Captain Voss sailed around the world. How he did it in such an un-seagoing canoe, I'll never know.

That evening at the Empress Hotel we met a couple from North Carolina. In the course of our conversation the wife mentioned that her maiden name was Plimsoll, I presume because I talked about ships. I told her the only Plimsoll I had heard was the chap who devised the load-line marking for saltwater ships. "That was my grandfather who was then a member of the House of Parliament!"

Needless to say the chance of meeting the granddaughter of the "father of the Plimsoll mark" will always be a memory of this shipman.

The Hazard of Sail

When browsing around in an old scrapbook I found this terrible tale from a clipping of the Vermilion paper dated June 13, 1889:

A Horrible Death
Captain Trinter, of the *Onoko*, killed in accident.

A telegraphic dispatch to Prof. C. G. Swensburg yesterday announced the death of Captain Wm. J. Trinter, of the steamer *Onoko*. When forty miles out from Ashland, while directing the hoisting of canvas, his overcoat caught in the drum of the pony and his body was drawn under the hoisting line. The drum made four revolutions before the machinery could be stopped, crushing the skull at each revolution.

Captain Trinter was a cousin of Prof. Swensburg. He had $40,000 interest in the *Onoko*, and $60,000 more in other iron steamers. The *Onoko* is the largest steamer on the lakes, and is principally owned by Captain P. G. Minch, Prof. Swensburg's uncle. Captain Trinter has been a well-known captain since he was twenty years old.

Ode to Commodore John G. Robinson on Reaching the Fathomless Age of 100

He was always lugging a large Graflex camera and taking snaps of boats and people he knew.

This was the tail-end of the "golden age" of yachting—magnificent yachts and memorable sailors.

John G. knew almost every yachtsman and boat on Lake Erie.

In later years he knew many powerboaters and boaters in the U. S. and Canada; especially speedboaters of the American Power Boat Association.

Why? Because John G. was the editor of Power Boating, a magazine published by Penton of Cleveland.

Not only was he an editor, he was also a fine writer, yachtsman, raconteur, gentleman, boat lover, cruiser, mechanic, marine historian, and everything else you can imagine about boats.

He was a boatman's boatman.

John grew up in Toronto and on Lake Ontario where he sailed and raced power and sail.

His first taste of internal combustion was on his cousin Bid's launch in 1902 at the Soo where a wonderful one-lunger moved them along with a gas vaporizer, make-and-break igniter and a sal ammoniac battery.
Then, when marine engines became somewhat more reliable, John went into powerboat racing on Toronto Bay.

He became a Great Lakes champion with his "V"-bottom displacement *Marco III* at about 30 miles per hour.

He introduced the famous Hall-Scott engine to the East.

So John was a real pioneer in the development and use of the marine engine.

Some of his cruising boats were *Minolta II, Consort I, II, III, IV,* and*V* and his last one, the *Crusoe (Robinson).*

In my mind's eye I can still see John G. with his Graflex walking along the docks at Put-in-Bay or Vermilion snapping shots of boats.

He was always happy, congenial, friendly, conversant and willing to talk boats to any man alive.

If a man can review his life and say, I saw everything in boats for ninety years on the Great Lakes, that man is Commodore John G. Robinson.

A great Canadian-American and a yachtsman to be remembered.

He will be missed.

Geo. P. Wakefield

Sloops and Bloops

One member of our Ship Admiring and Watching Society way out west in Victoria, B.C., went straight up through the deck hatch and then over the side when I ineptly called Captain Voss's *Tillicum* a sloop. Jim Davis didn't exactly know what the rig was, but he knew it wasn't a sloop so he called the specialists at the museum and found it to be a "three-masted bastard rigged ketch with a single clubbed heads'l."

So much for proper nomenclature. I am still somewhat aghast to think of going to sea in such a boat. Voss and Captain Slocum of the famous *Spray* were rugged sailors to circumnavigate the earth in such small sailboats. It is good to have the *Tillicum* preserved at the museum as a fine specimen of long distance sailers. The *Spray* disappeared at sea.

Thanks, Jim. You are now captain of the NW Section of the exclusive SAWS. You are especially commended for your alertness in reading the *Inland Seas* and intense love to keep "Lure" in Bristol fashion. I ran into another blooper last month: *Cutty Sark* was described as a schooner because she has "lots of sails." Another "laker", no doubt, who grew up with schooner yarns.

Sleek Sephie docked at the lumber yard in Kincardine, Ont., in 1900, a fast schooner of the years. Photo by Ron Beaupre of Port Elgin, Ont.

Sephie

The first time I saw *Sephie* was in a store window on the square in Goderich, a photo of her at the dock in the harbor under full sail. Since a fair breeze was blowing I was curious about why she was "sailing" at the dock with mains, topsails and jibs drawing?

This was an unusual situation—a three-master sailing hard tied to the dock; so I have pondered over what actually had taken place in the faraway years of the nineties. Had they been trying her new sails and were caught by an unexpected wind? Surely she seemed to be in a bad predicament for how could they lower sails under pressure of the wind with the canvas against the dock? Your guess is as good as mine unless you have the answer. My conclusions come from some experience with small sailboats so the apparent problems with schooner sails are amplified considerably. I expect we'll never have an answer to this perplexity, but I did find out more about the good ship.

This fine three-master was built by Joseph Williams in 1889 for the lumber trade of Henry Malton on Ship Island in Goderich Harbor. In case you start looking for it, the island was removed in 1962. Mr. Kenneth Hunter, C.T.E. commissioner of works for the city, supplied this information to me in Goderich's Sesquicentennial booklet, *Memories of Goderich*, which he so generously forwarded. Ron Beaupre of Port Elgin furnished the clear picture of the *Sephie* docked in Kincardine harbor about 1900.

The *Sephie* a was fine looking lake schooner with a graceful sheer, nicely curved stem and a beautiful counter. The rig was typical for a fast sailer with tall topmasts for ample tops'ls for light going. I note she didn't carry a yard at the foremast (commonly called a rafee) which kept her rig simple for the lumber trade.

In the photo at Kincardine it is not clear whether she is loading lumber or discharging it. Perhaps local historians can clarify this for us. I know, though, the lumber mill has disappeared from the harbor to the extent that not a vestige remains of a busy industry on the banks of the Penetangore River.

Nothing stands but the quaint lighthouse that has become a memory of the past in that pleasant little harbor on Lake Huron.

Port of Vermilion

Rick Wright of the Institute of Great Lakes Research at Bowling Green State University provided the following detail of arrival and departures at Port Vermilion where the Great Lakes Historical Society Inland Seas Museum is located:

Steamer *Commerce*: built in Sandusky, Ohio, in 1837 by Daniel Dibble. Dimensions: 74'x 17'61"x 6'9"; 78 69/95 tons. Abandoned in 1898.

Schooner *Express*: built at Avon, Ohio, in 1837, 2 masts. Dimensions: 72'23"x 19'8"x 6'4"; 64 04/95 tons.

Scow Schooner *Sarah Jane*: built at Irving, N. Y,. in 1832 by Charles Huntley, 2 masts. Dimensions: 64'11"x 14'6"x 4'5"; 37 25/95 tons.

Schooner *New York*: built in Cleveland, Ohio, in 1834 by Waterman Ells, 2 masts. Dimensions: 60'11"x 18'x 5'11"; 56 22/95 tons.

Schooner *Josephine*: built in Sandusky, Ohio, in 1832, 2 masts. Dimensions: 50'4"x 16'3"x6'3"; 43 76/95 tons.

Sloop *Great western:* not listed in vessel enrollments.

These vessels were all small of shallow draft for crossing bars at river mouths, some without piers. Another 40 years would spell doom for the little harbor as the ships grew too large.

Commercial fishing lasted to 1980, the end of an era. But pleasure boaters took up the slack with 1,700 calling the river home port and thousands more visiting via lake and trailer. What would the early settlers have thought of that? It was an unimagined destiny. What a transformation—hard work to easy fun!

Old wooden steamer Toledo, built in 1863 with an early, cranky steam engine.

The Longest Back

Many of our readers have not seen this story of how the steamer *Toledo* backed into history. Therefore I have lifted it from the Inland Seas of April 1945 because it is such a gem.

The oldtimer, *Toledo*, a wooden steamer built in 1863, had a single-cylinder engine with wooden supports columns and some strange contrivance in the way of reversing gear overhead made fast to the deck. It was because of this that it took both engineers to operate it.

You get the picture, and here is what happened as related by Captain England when he boarded his first ship as a watchman.

"At last we got the old ship painted and the sails bent and we were ready for sea. The ship was lying in a slip at the lower end of Detroit. When the captain gave the signal to back, she backed and never stopped until she landed on the river bank at Sandwich, Canada. The captain was busy giving signals and using bad language. Fortunately as she backed out into the current, she backed upstream a bit, landing port side to. A tug pulled her off, and we proceeded to Hurley's coal dock to take on fuel.

"Captain Eber Ward, the owner, met us and the lurid talk that followed was classic. It was our captain's first year on the *Toledo*, and he much resented being on a ship that would not stop when he wanted her to do so. Captain Ward would not entertain at all the demand for a new engineer, saying that the old men were the only ones who could run her. Finally they made some repairs to the engine and I always had the impression some were made to the engineer too. This was my first experience with an indispensable engineer."

Told by Captain R. W. England.

River Sounds

Someone blowing a boiler out with high pressure steam whistling away, drowning out all other sounds.

The *Edward K.* in a fog off Vermilion with her deep throated whistle tootin' at intervals.

Old Gib's *Owl* barking spasmodically doing her best to keep going.

Or the noisiest gas boat in the river, the *John N.*, with her two cylinder Vim—no muffler!

And Cloudy's *Gertrude* perking away very politely.

Gas boats going out in the morning with their identifying exhausts.

A steamer under forced draft sounding like a panting swimmer.

A bell or whistle from an anxious skipper coming to the dock.

Puffing from a non-condensor that is music to the ears.

Or the thunder under the stern from a throbbing propeller.

The thud of empty fish boxes being piled on deck.

Enthusiastic crewmen unloading fish and their happy voices.

Coal being shoveled aboard ship or tumbling from chute to deck.

The reeling of nets and the song from wooden bearings.

Carp spawning in the marsh grass. Gulls screaming over cast-off fish.

A boat being built in old George's shed. A safety valve popping when she checks.

Kids swimming at the pumphouse board. Someone calling a dog, "Here Rex, here Rex, yut, yut, yut."

Three Great Story Tellers of the Great Lakes

My lament about these three super story tellers is that we knew them well and yet we did not have the foresight to record their choice bits of history when we could have done so. However, perhaps someone out there has partially recorded them, and would forward the stories to "Lure of the Lakes."

Captain Lew Stone was a fine spinner of yarns and might have been the Mark Twain of the lakes if he had taken the time to write, but he didn't, so we have been the losers. He had the gift and humor of Sam Clemens and the experience to go along, but he lacked the incentive to put it down in script. The captain's pet artifact beside his chair in the pilothouse was his shining brass cuspidor. I heard from some members of the crew who had the pleasure of sailing with this witty character that the Cap was an expert shot, too. I do know that his Hudson Super-Six was equipped with a similar container, and as his wife drove him around town like a chauffeur, I often saw him in the act of "shootin' the target."

Another expert at lake stories was Captain Herb Dosey, a former vice-president of the society and chairman of the museum committee. Herb's background was electric interurban railways, yachting and steamboating. He told the gamut of life's experiences with the memory of a computer and the natural skill of a professional entertainer. Herb could imitate the air compressor on a "Greenline" car like the real thing. I have found that skill of such nature identifies a superfan. Trouble is, we lost Herb Dosey in the fragility of voice and memory. This is a passing salute to Herb.

Captain Chelsey Inches, another grand raconteur I had the great pleasure of knowing well, knew every ship on the Great Lakes by name, place of building and date; and more if you wanted. Since he lived in the wooden ship days he was a schooner and steamer expert. He corrected me when I mentioned lumber "hooker"; the proper description was lumber carrier.

One story about Captain Lew Stone was his favorite:

Captain Jones was touched with fear of heavy weather. Possibly he had been truly frightened on Superior and had come near losing his ship, which would be excusable under certain circumstances. At any rate, Captain Stone knew this light-hearted skipper well and knew of his tendency to duck in from big seas. Cap Stone was considered a heavy weather man and pushed his vessel to keep her on schedule. One exceedingly brutal day on Superior, Cap Stone remarked to his wheelsman, "You know, I don't know where old Jones is today but I sure wish I was there!"

It must have been some blow.

Tall Ships in a Little Harbor

Last fall we were surprised to see a real live sailing ship enter our harbor. She was large, 162 feet overall with spars reaching to the sky some 100 feet, and yards spreading like gull wings. She was the three-masted bark, *Merkur*, out of Merry Olde England making the round of Great Lake ports. It is not often (if ever) that a bark lays over at little Vermilion (Lake Erie) sporting a red duster at her mizzen. She docked at the old schooner launching berth in view of the museum, so the event sparked reflections among ship-history buffs.

From that very location Vermilion's contributions to lake transportation in the years between 1840 and 1880 reached a peak with the launching of 51 large ships which developed a host of lake sailors. In 1919 we could boast of a greater number of lake captains per capita than any other community on the lakes. Those days passed, though, with the coming of steam and steel plates. The per capita of ship historians has diminished, too, to a rare few since the coming of Ford workers to the ex-schooner town. Newcomers were mostly inlanders who wouldn't know the difference between a boom and a bowsprit.

But *Merkur's* spars in the sky provided just the touch of yesterday to help us imagine the harbor of a century ago with four or five schooners at the dock. It was a thrill to see the *Merkur*. Best wishes to the ship and the crew in their wanderings around the world from the little harbor that remembers.

While the *Merkur* was an attraction, she did not create excitement like the *Thomas Quale* did in 1920 when practically the whole town came to the foot of Huron Street to see her. The big barge with her two tall spars came in for repair of her port bow after bashing the pier at Toledo. Due to the shortage of shipping on the lakes from the ship drain caused by U-boats of WWI, anything that could carry cargo was pumped out and put to work.

Why Vermilion?

We still had a gaggle of ship carpenters in town and they were hungry and willing to patch anything wooden. Most of them were tobacco chewing and cussing raconteurs. But they were the tail-end of the shipyard crew of the '80s and they knew how to work wooden ships. Of them, I knew Jim Brooks and "Pop" Nichols and often listened to their ship yarns. Their faces and characteristics still linger in my mind. In no time, it seemed, the ten-foot hole was patched and the old hull was caulked and painted.

One personal incident I well recall was during a conversation we boys had at the dock with the old man who was going to take the *Quayle* out. It took place while we were watching two workers caulking the topsides.

"When will the corkers be finished?" I innocently asked.

The captain chuckled and rubbed his head, "You're the corker." The fun we had scampering aboard the *Quayle* must have been reported to him by the watchman because our rampages just about drove him batty. But isn't that what kids have done over the centuries?

The Thinning Crowd

December 29, 1985, 11 a.m.: The last lake ship passed by today. It was a Great Lakes Towing tug running east through the ice flows for the winter lay-up, I presume. This reminds me of the twenties when lake ships were as common as yachts today along our waterfront. Those small ships with their accompanying smoke tails streaming on the horizon were a daily sight along Vermilion way and we miss them. Walter Havinghurst's romantic title, *Long Ships Passing,* has another connotation these days; it is one of passing away since the 200- to 650-footers are all but gone. Seldom do we see a1000-footer in close; when we do we are all eyes. A few 730s go into Huron and these we relish with binoculars as they sail silently past. Occasionally a few years ago, we would see a ship heading in for Vermilion and realize the skipper was picking up the Huron landfall, because the course was about the same as that for Huron on the long trip from Buffalo or Port Colborne. As it turned, we chuckled over his inability to distinguish the difference between residential Vermilion and our commercialized neighbor to the west.

Wooden Ships and Seams

A wooden ship is a different animal from our steel lakers. First, when you board one you know she is wooden from the strips of lumber in the topsides, the trademark of ships over the ages. They were built that way because wood was the only material available. How to plug the seam to keep the water out has always been a problem. The seam was critical. Just about everything imaginable has been used to jam between the abutting planks but none was totally sufficient. Basically they either leaked slowly at the dock and required regular pump-out or they failed miserably in large seas, accounting for loss of life. "Man the pumps!" was the hated and back-breaking command at sea, but it had to be done. It was a sink or swim situation. Building ships, not small boats, of wood was about as sensible as making a balloon of animal skins.

Walking the deck of a wooden ship produced a muffled sound, a direct contrast to the clink, clink on steel ships. And steelers have little aroma other than the paint whereas wood is either fresh or rotting, either odor quickly identifiable. The texture of the wooden ship and the monolithic appearance of steel plate strike another contrast. But steel held the answer to the seams' vulnerability—the non-leaking plate and the positive welded joint. What an improvement, revolutionary!

While thinking of the caulking work on the *Quayle*, I remembered the technique I viewed as a youngster: men worked in pairs supported on a raft alongside. First, the seam was cleared of old material; one man then roughly inserted the rolled oakum with a caulking tool and a mallet, the other worker completed the first stage. One held the caulking iron by a metal handle, the maul

Old wooden schooner Thomas Quayle reduced to a schooner barge in Vermilion port for repair. Photo: Institute for Great Lakes Research, Bowling Green University.

man hit hard to put the oakum home. Last they used a thick paint to cover the visible oakum. The resounding ring of steel on steel of the repair team was music in the ears of ship folk. The aroma of tarred oakum permeated the fo'c'sle of all wooden ships.

Another memory of the *Quayle* was the dark, dank and dismal sight and smell as I peered down into the water-filled hold of a dying ship—the last of her breed. It left me with a definite chill. But the musical anvil chorus of the caulking irons ringing throughout the valley still lingers in my mind as a lovely memory of the days when ships were built of wood.

Fish and Tips

In 1927 Roy Grant was sailing as porter on the *Empire City* with Captain Charlie Horton. The *Empire City* was one of the high-power ships of the Pittsburgh Steamship Company used for towing a consort. In this trip it was the barge *Manila* sailed by "Brocky" Young. The two ships left Duluth loaded with ore for Conneaut in a strong westerly that increased as they moved downlake. Later, when he walked aft, Roy said, "The towering seas astern would advance as giants of green water and the ship would raise her fantail and let them pass like the old gal she was."

But then there was trouble when the barge signaled the danger salute of rapid toots from her steam whistle. The steam winch had broken and they were pulling off bollards in the frantic task of holding the cable, so the *Empire* had to slow down or lose the barge completely. In the excitement and confusion from the lack of good communication between vessels, the ships got into the troughs and shifted their cargoes. Captain Horton decided to put into the lee of Keeweenaw and straighten up. It took three days of snatch blocks, scoop shovels and windlasses, plus a lot of hard work by the crews who all pitched in to save the ships. Roy ran the aft winch in the rush.

In the delay, food became scarce and an Indian fisherman must have known it. He came along side with a fine catch of lake trout. Roy supervised the purchase of several fine fish, the smallest being 17 pounds.

Roy later left the lakes but still vividly remembers the drama of the big seas, the tipped cargo and those beautiful lake trout!

Paddle Wheels and Cross-chains

The Ohio River Museum at Marietta is a dandy. The history of river steamboating is on display there in artifacts, pictures and a real steamer, the *W. P. Snyder, Jr*. At first glance, a laker has somewhat of a shock at seeing the low freeboard of a river ship, I mean boat, but on further inspection I was duly impressed with her good functional design and construction. A shipman would be delighted to poke around on this vessel for she is a novel sight.

Up for'd is the coal bunker with two screw stokers feeding the twin boilers. Then a mid-ship gangway separates the engine room from the boilers. The engines are on each side mounted horizontally, connected to the big paddle wheel at the stern via a wooden beam. The engines appear to be of the steeple type compounded for improved efficiency, very massive for slow turning. The crew quarters are above the engines affording some respite, no doubt, from the boiler beat. Up for'd is the pilothouse done in plain fashion compared to the old gingerbread types; still, the tempo fits into the overall boat design nicely. I noted the forward window without glass was well protected with adjustable shields, a method of providing the pilot with an unobstructed view in all weather free from glass reflections. This technique was apparently common on riverboats, a bit unusual perhaps, but very practical as long as the pot-bellied stove just aft of the wheelsman kept burning merrily along.

That night we watched a couple of diesel tugs go rumbling upstream with tows ahead, lit up like old passenger boats. The *Snyder* with her rugged paddle wheel astern didn't seem to pay any attention to the modern screw boats with their Kort nozzles and electronic equipment. We did notice, though, the definite lack of sonorous whistle blowing which is always exciting to shipmen; perhaps due to radio communication which was missing on the *Snyder*. Another traditional musical note gone gaily west.

At Zaneville we boarded a live stern wheeler for a short voyage on the Muskingum River. She was the *Lorena,* an old steamer built in Hamar, Ohio, (where?) in 1895, now with a diesel with chain drive on her paddle. From her I learned about old river boats; for instance, to maneuver you have to back? The rudders are ahead of the paddle wheel so to put current on the rudder the old man must back her. This sort of cross-chain effect when viewed ahead causes somewhat of a state of confusion to a Great Laker, but one gets used to unfamiliar motion in time.

This all reminds me of Paul Tappan's Downeaster he brought to the lakes in the twenties. She was a fifty-foot schooner, *Diana*, equipped with the usual saltwater steering rig, cross-chain. One day they were running down from the Islands in a strong westerly going great guns. Dette Parsons was aboard as wheelsman. Now Dette was an old hand at steering anything on the lakes and was skipper of the *J. Burton Ayers* of the Great Lakes Steamship Company. They came into the pier full speed and how Dette mastered that cross-chain confusion in that critical spot was a sight to see. It was all over his face, the tenseness of steering. I don't think he fully recovered until Paul dropped the canvas in the safety of the river. Were lake schooners cross-chain? I'll bet they were from the influence of the Downeasters and their shipbuilding methods.

A note about how I used to steer a cross-chainer: I sat beside the wheel and pretended I was steering with a tiller! Problem solved for a tiller, you turn towards your self and the bow goes the other way. Easy going!

The *W. P. Snyder, Jr.*, a Pittsburgh type river steamer, part of the Ohio River Museum at Marietta, Ohio. Courtesy of the Ohio River Museum.

DEAR EDITOR:

Just like to make a few comments on George P. Wakefield's article on the Str. *W. P. Snyder, Jr.*. (Everyone likes to show how smart they are. Hope Mr. Wakefield will excuse me.) The *Snyder* is an example of a "pool" type towboat. Her pilothouse was for'd and low and the stacks (funnels) were counterbalanced and hinged and could be lowered to pass under low bridges. This type boat was developed in the Pittsburgh area. Lower river towboats had their pilothouse amidships, on top of the cabin structure and their stacks were higher.

The shield on the for'd side of the pilothouse was called a breast board and was usually adjustable.

Sternwheel boats had an engine on each side, directly connected to the wheel with cranks at 90 degrees. The *Snyder* had tandem compound engines (high and low pressure on each side on a common piston rod), and was condensing. The connecting rod, known as a pitman, was usually of oak with a steel frame with jaws for the bearings at each end.

As these engines were long stroke (up to 12 feet) and slow (20 RPM) they usually had balanced poppet valves operated by cams, and very positive cut-offs. On later boats the cams were turned by tumbling bars operated off the pitman. The cut-off was variable and was actuated by the crosshead.

The tows these boats could handle were almost unbelievable. One boat I worked on, the *Omar*, had engines 16"x 32"x8' stroke. Her paddle wheel was 24'x24' with 48 buckets. We never left Huntington with less than 21 barges and a fuel flat. This gave us a tow approximately 1,100 feet long and 104 feet wide. This was the largest tow that could be locked through in two sections. On an open river, when the dams were down, we would handle up to thirty barges.

The technique of steering by putting the rudders hard down and going astern, was known as "flanking" and was very effective. Sometimes with a big tow on an open river, we would start going astern at New Richmond, Ohio, to land the tow at Addyston, Ohio, a distance of some thirty miles.

The largest sternwheel towboat ever built was the *Sprague*. Her engines were 32" x 64" x 12' stroke. She once took a load of coal covering 3.5 acres to New Orleans.

Hope this will give you some idea of a different kind of steamboating. Those old paddle wheelers were simple, effective and easy to maintain. Some of their engines lasted 100-130 years.

I was an engineer on these boats before going to saltwater and also worked on one of the big side wheelers with independent engines. Hope this isn't boring. I have rambled long enough so will ring off.

Don Naish
ex-chief engineer
3854 Crawford Road
Dryden, MI 48428

When the Ice Goes Out

When the ice goes out in the old home town, things begin to move,

Up and away in the spring air, out of the deep ice groove.

The last piles of snow are melting down to the sleeping grass

Leaving all that remains of last winter's blasts.

Blackbirds and crows are about, chirping happily as rabbits leap

Across a gurgling drain rolling rapidly to creek.

And the fishermen are active as the tugs go out to set;

Their hopes are for perch as they stream a perfect net.

The ice along shore has a sullen mood with wind and sand

Covering it's once white surface which now looks like land.

The grass is flat and soggy waiting for a week of sun

To vitalize the blades and start the chlorophyll to run.

The trees are still in winter trim, showing all their form

Of trunks, branches, twigs, and buds set in the ground forlorn.

But Vermilionites are happy after a long winter bout

And it's all because we love it when the ice goes out.

A Tribute to Admiral Bayfield

One hundred and fifteen years ago Admiral Henry Wolsey Bayfield passed away in Charlottetown, Prince Edward Island, at the age of 90. This pioneer Great Lakes surveyor of the Royal Navy left many a charted shoreline, island, bay, rock and depth to eternity. Then a young lieutenant in the British Navy, he surveyed Lake Erie in 1818, Lake Huron and Georgian Bay from 1819 to 1822, and Lake Superior by the end of 1825. He spent his entire life in the navy, charting virgin areas so man could navigate in safety. From 1827 to 1856 inclusive, he and his staff surveyed the entire Gulf of St. Lawrence, Prince Edward Island, Newfoundland and Nova

Scotia. This task consumed 29 years. Bayfield was a gentleman of intelligence, perseverance, scientific skill and the inquisitiveness of an explorer. We of the lakes owe this naval man a time honored place in history of the Great Lakes for his almost superhuman efforts in remote and wild seascapes which he transmitted with the minimum of equipment and assistance. For a glimpse into his task here is a letter* he wrote to his chief, Admiral Beaufort:

"Two boats not larger than ships cutters carried our whole stock of conveniences, of which we had fewer than the native Indians. Officers and men shared alike, for the Boats would not admit of our taking more with us than a change of clothes. I had not room for even of a mattress, but slept in all weathers, in the Boat, or on the shore upon a Buffalo robe under the Boat's main sail thrown over a few branches placed on the ground. Many a night have we slept out, in this way, when the Thermometer was down to near zero, and sometimes below it. Yet even this was not so wearing as trying to sleep in vain, in warm nights of summer (when the Thermometer was at 80 degrees) in the smoke of a fire to keep off the clouds of Moschetoes which literally darkened the air, fatigued as we generally were from sitting from sunrise to sunset in our open Boats... and when this occurred the Ague, or other sickness was sure to make it's appearance among us."

Admiral Bayfield will always be remembered for his copious journals from the hand of a prolific scribe, and the natural memorials in his charted areas named Bayfield.

**With kind permission of The Champlain Society in Toronto.*

SAWS Report

Had a nice call from Dick Palmer, one of our senior editors, and he had a logical explanation of the good ship *Sephie* of Goderich sailing at the dock under full canvas. She was drying her sails! It may have been that simple. On the other hand, possibly she was trying her new sails when the wind came along and put her on the starboard tack in the unusual predicament of sailing at the dock. I figured she was doing about six miles per.

Dick is a member of the SAWS (Ship Admiring and Watching Society) and a specialist in lake schooners and history on Lake Ontario. He told me that Oswego, New York, must have built 300 schooners in the building years, 1810 to 1880, and from that information may take the honors as the champion builder of schooners on the lakes. From reports of Pierce McClouth of Marine City, Michigan, and the history of the town, Marine City built some 250 wooden ships in her heyday which in itself is some sort of a record. Any challengers?

Chasin' A Captain

We were laying over one night in Marine City in the quiet waters of the Belle River after a salmon fishing expedition in Lake Huron. Didn't catch any, but we Lake Erieians were thrilled to stream a bait in the crystal water of Huron because of its shocking transparency.

Mary and I walked to town from our berth at Stave Point and noticed the old town showing the signs of the times in contrast to yesteryear when the town boasted more freighter sailors than any town on the Great Lakes. Before the turn of the century when small ships were in wild profusion, Marine City was rightfully named; in the spring two passenger trains transported the crews, skippers and engineers to Duluth for fitting out.

I had another mission, though, to meet Captain Byron Stuart, an old friend of Captain Inches of the museum. They were school pals at Algonac back in the 80s. Captain Inches once told me, in one of his many story telling sessions, that he often rowed across the river to Harsens Island and ferried Byron back to school.

Stopping at a nearby house I inquired where to find Captain Stuart. The lady replied, "Why he was just here. There he goes now, off to the post office." So we went in pursuit. He was in his late eighties and scooting through town like a deer. We finally caught up with him and introduced ourselves. When he heard we were friends of Chelsey Inches it made us his friends.

We had a very pleasant chat with the old sea dog about ships and days of yore. Then we had to go. Since we were going back to Inches country, Bryon handed us a letter he happened to have for Captain Inches.

As we said goodbye to the veteran Great Laker we noticed an expression of delight which we suspected had nothing to do with us. The old rascal had saved a stamp!

KISS

From the quarterly of the National Maritime Historical Society, *Sea History*, come some nicknames of naval vessels created by the ever active moniker section of a navy. Here are some British examples that tongue tied the sailors: *Hermione, Penelope, Bacchante* and *Bellerophon.* So we have:

"Hermy-one," "Penny-lope," "Bag-shanty," "Bully-ruffian." You can't stop sailors from simplifying the language.

The general axiom for sailors around the world must surely be: "Keep it simple, Sailor."

On the lakes we have the "Soo" for Sault St. Marie, "Snye" for Chanel Ecarte and "Snow" for Les Chanaux Islands. There must be many more. What do you have to offer?

The Captain's Kid

Both of my parents were originally from central New York State so they planned a vacation trip to visit the old homestead, traveling from Cleveland to Buffalo by boat. I was about three, and not knowing how I would take life on the boat my folks watched me pretty closely.

However on one occasion I managed to sneak away from the family. My anxious parents started searching and asking others if they had seen a red-headed girl. Suddenly all the kids on the boat seemed to have red hair. The search finally took my parents to the pilothouse where they found the doors, as usual, locked. They rapped on the window to report the missing child, and there I was on the Captain's lap!

For many years afterwards, I intended to become a lady captain of the *Seeandbee*. I guess I was two generations too early for a sailing career, but I have certainly enjoyed my close association with the marine business for over 30 years, begun by the Captain of the *Seeandbee*.

Submitted by Virginia Walsh, Cleveland, Ohio.

Sounds in the Night

We spent a vacation in a cottage by the sea near Newagen, Maine, on a peninsula below Boothbay Harbor. For some strange reason I dreamed of trains going by every night which was very unusual on the oceanfront miles away from trains.

When we came back home the whole mystery unraveled one night lying in bed—the New York Central locomotive racing by and blowing for the crossings had the same whistle blasts as the foghorn on the Cuckolds, an island off our cottage in Maine!

They had to be identical horns to sound the same and I presume they were. Could they have been Kahlenberg horns made in Two Rivers, Wisconsin?

Vim, Vigor and Pride

In 1916 Cliff Parsons was fishing with his first powered gill-netter, *Pride*, out of Vermilion. One day out near the International Line north of home port the lubrication failed and burned out the connecting rod bearing on the first cylinder of his two-cylinder Vim gasoline engine.

What to do now? Well, Cliff was an ingenious chap full of get-up and go, plus an overabundance of perseverance. He was in a pickle with not a boat in sight to tow him in. He thought for awhile and the answer to his dilemma was to try to get the old motor to "mote" again. Cliff got out his tools and went to work. He removed the cylinder head and lifted it from the piston; disconnected the burned out bearing and removed the piston and rod from the crankshaft; he then put back the head and started the engine on the back cylinder and brought the *Pride* back to port!

The Sandusky-made Vim was never meant to operate on "one lung" but Cliff Parsons made it work and that is one reason why he became a very successful commercial fisherman.

Told to me by Cliff Parsons in 1976 when he was 90 years old.

The Last Sail

It was 1939 when my brother Fred chartered the two-masted schooner, *Northwest*, an old Toronto stone carrier, and sold passages to the annual Inter-Lake Yachting Association Regatta at Put-in Bay. On sailing day an excited crew of "romantic historians," all yachtsmen, boarded the ship at the foot of Huron Street, the old shipyard site. With the usual "good bye" and "happy sailing" salutations we felt like sailors of the 1880s shipping out for Duluth. In a fair NE breeze we made sail off the Vermilion lighthouse and headed NW for the bay. We had a ball hauling and coiling lines and imagining we were real tars. It was a grand adventure and a privilege for all hands.

It wasn't our fault that the skipper-owner knew nothing about sailing for that didn't faze us one fathom as we were all "windjammers" from the keel-boat racing fleet. His ineptitude merely made more fun for us.

After a rare time at the bay we made sail off Ballast Island and started for home. While passing north of Kelly Island we set our rhumb line for Vermilion port which was invisible in the long thin blue line of the south shore. The wind was fresh from the NE and the *Northwest*, close-hauled, was racing to the SE like a spirited horse racing home. About a mile off shore we had to tack to the east to make the harbor, but she wouldn't answer her helm! Here we were going hell-bent for the beach and we couldn't do a thing to keep her from piling up on the Main Street beach (right at the GLHS Museum). Right at the last minute, before we stove in the waterworks intake crib, she came about!

One of the smart sailors had lowered the centerboard and the *Northwest* responded as she was supposed to do. As I mentioned at the start, it was our first sail on a Great Lakes schooner. We now know how to sail ships of her breed but where are we going to get another chance to prove our skills? What a thrill it was to sail the *Northwest*, the last of the lake schooners. To all those hands who sailed her that memorable day, she is gone but not forgotten—just, "gone with the wind."

A Hayseed's Quandary

A quip in the Winter *Inland Seas* 1981 "Lure" reminds me of another barnyard story from my family. In the mid-twenties my mother (then a recent graduate of business college) came east after growing up in Arizona and California. She had an office job, and worked for her room and board with a friendly family in East Cleveland. A number of times she heard a sound somewhat familiar to her ears, but since it was an urban area, couldn't quite figure it out. So she finally asked her "family" if there were any farms nearby. Why? —because she kept hearing the cries of a cow that had just lost her calf. No one could imagine what she was referring to and decided it must be her imagination because there were certainly no cows in East Cleveland.

The sounds came to her over and over, and she would even catch herself looking at grassy spots around billboards to see if a cow was tied up to graze. Sometime later, the "cries" finally came when everyone was at supper. The group was quickly hushed, and moments later the foghorn sounded again! After the laughter died down, and the explanation was given, her red face toned back to normal, and supper in the big city went on as usual. But, of course, she never lived it down!

Told by Virginia Walsh, Cleveland, Ohio.

A Bell Bottom Venture

When I was a youngster around fourteen, along the waterfront, my brother Ernie built an "experimental" diving hood out of someone's metal wastebasket. He puttied in a piece of glass and weighted it with a "necklace" of gill-net leads. The air equipment consisted of a boat gas tank and a bicycle pump with a suitable piece of garden hose.

Coincidentally, George Parsons of Vermilion had picked up a net anchor in one of his wheels on his 55-foot gill-netter *Mary F. II*. He had heard rumors about the "kid's diving bell" and since he didn't relish running his boat to Sandusky for a haul-out, he contacted Ernie for help.

We all gathered around the tug to see the great diving bell trial. Someone in the gang suggested that I take it down which I did with a lot of perturbation for it had never been tried! George put a line on me just in case he had to yank me out and up. I succeeded and when I came up I was an instant hero; I was the first guy to go to the bottom of the Vermilion River in an inverted wastebasket!

Fisherman's Luck

This is another Parsons' story. The family settled in Vermilion in 1810 when Solomon Parsons moved from Roxbury, Delaware County, New York. He built one of the first schooners, the *Vermilion*, in 1814 and since that time eight generations of Parsons have grown up along the river. Hence it is not unusual to expect many stories to include the Parsons boys for the yarns follow like a ship's wake.

Nelson Parsons fished the steel trap-netter *Don* out of Vermilion in the forties and often told of his narrow escape from death in the lake. He and his crew were fishing off the port one morning when a dense "pea-souper" came in and caught them unawares some several miles out in the lake. Now, Nel's engine was a very reliable Chrysler which never failed to start on the first turn of the switch. With visibility down to the boat length of 30 feet, he finished dipping fish from the pot and started in. The first turn of the switch failed to start the "old reliable" for the first time and in that very next second a freighter swooshed past his bow going full speed! If the engine had started as it always had, Nelson would have been smashed and sunk squarely in the beam by the ship's bow. I guess that is why Nel always swore by those Chrysler engines!

The Finish Gun

My favorite yachting story is about the *Shark*, the Vermilion Boat Club tender, and my brother Fred. The boat was a 30-foot glass cabin cruiser that had formerly served in the same capacity for the Cleveland Yacht Club in the early twenties. She came to VBC in the thirties after being owned by Dr. Culp of Rocky River as his cruiser. In her later years she towed the Star boats of VBC to the annual Inter-Lake regattas at Put-In Bay and served as a "home" for many of the Star boat crews.

One year, while anchored out in the lee of Gibraltar Island with the gang aboard, the island flies attacked like hungry beasts and if you have experienced their "bite-ability" you will understand why Fred took the most unusual means to rid the old *Shark* of these monsters. He decided to burst their lungs by concussion! Since the flies were so active and the boys so irritated, they were quite willing to innovate, as swatting was ineffective. Fred, always ready with a new idea, cleared the cabin, shut all windows and placed the 10-gauge starting cannon in the center of the cabin on the engine housing; he next ran the gun lanyard under the door to the aft cockpit.

"All set? Here she goes," he piped, as he pulled the lanyard, followed by a blast that shook the ship from stem to stern. The gang was jubilant and let out a cheer that was heard from Peach Point to the Perry Monument. But you know, on checking up on the flies, they had all left—right through the windows for all the glass had gone to sea!

Told to me by Commodore H. Allen Hall in 1930.

A Seagoing Rail-Splitter

"Big Ed" Lampe was a famous Lake Erie gill-netter and a rare character in commercial fishing lore all over the lake for two basic reasons: One, he was a big fellow about 6'6" and strong as an ox. His feats of strength were renowned like a Paul Bunyan of the lakes. He looked like Abe Lincoln with deep lines in his face forming a sad expression coupled with a rawbone, lanky physique. Since he came from Lincoln country in Illinois he could have been a relative as he talked in a slow, backwoodsman's language. Secondly, Big Ed was an innovator in the things he did, like building a "round" ice house, a new type of fish boat, the early introduction of the gasoline engine, and the construction of a "push" type trawl. This is the background of our yarn about Big Ed.

One day while he was returning to port on the *Sidney & Wayne* he lost his steerage. The rudder had let go at the stuffing box and the boat was uncontrollable. His innovative mind went to work. At the stern he tossed overboard two net boxes with lines attached and, holding a line in each hand, he "reined" her into port! After docking, Big Ed said in his drawling, regional brogue, "Waal, it was just like drivin' a team of horses—backin'!"

Contributed by Geo. Roberts of Vermilion, Ohio (a Big Ed devotee).

Storm Terror

Captain Bob Parsons sailed the steamer *Thomas F. Cole* in 1940 and very luckily went through the big storm on Lake Michigan that year. He personally told me the following yarn about a porter.

We had a cook aboard the *Cole* who had brought along Andrew, a friend of his from the deep south who went to sea for the first time. Unfortunately, we got caught in the big blow and almost lost our ship on the east shore of Lake Michigan! It was the worst gale of my life on the lakes and it was a whistler. We finally made port in Milwaukee with 100,000 sheared or loose rivets and a smashed galley that looked like a giant stew.

No sooner had we made fast and put a ladder over when this porter came running up from aft with his suitcase. I talked to him when he was about to descend the ladder. "Where are you going, Andy? How come you are covered with white dust?" His reply in a very hurried and excited tone was, "I'm gettin' off this boat forever. She's too rough for me." And he left running up the dock and away.

The chap was so frantic from fear that he had spent most of the storm's duration in an asbestos barrel in the boiler room!

The Battle of the Valve

Alfred Buell was older than most recruits when he entered training at the Con Ed plant in New York City to learn the secrets of steam turbine operation in World War II. After graduating, he went to sea on an anti-aircraft light cruiser of the Atlanta class in the western Pacific.

The ship was steaming along at the usual 27 knots when a slow signal came down from the bridge; in the engine room all hell broke out from the high pressure steam escaping from the bleeder valve on the feed water tank. The room immediately became a cauldron of steam and noise and when you are all "dogged down" this is no fun. In the excitement, the chief, who was an old reciprocating engineer drafted from the merchant fleet, ran to the turbine exhaust valve and started to close it; Buell knew this was the wrong way so wrested the valve from the chief and opened it! The steaming ceased.

Later in port, the chief standing beside the executive engineering officer, pointed to Buell and said, "See that fellow, Buell, he knows more about running this engine room than anyone." To get even with "rascal" Buell, the chief sent him to the bilge to hose it clean. When the chief came down to inspect the cleanup, Buell accidentally "wet him down" which was sweet revenge for knowing too much about turbine operation on the *USS Flint*! Subsequently, Buell was threatened to be put on report by the chief but Buell pulled out his notebook of "Dumb Acts by the Chief" and the case was closed.

Two conclusions follow: the Con Ed plant did a good job of teaching, and Buell was too old for the engine room on the good ship *Flint*!

Told to me by Alfred Buell of Vermilion, Ohio, ex Machinist Mate 2nd Class, USS Flint.

Yesterday's Boater

Charlie Robertson was in his late seventies when I first knew him along the riverfront in the twenties. I was a young lad about eight with a strong, intense interest in boats and engines. Any power boat in the river was fair game to satisfy my craving to get my hands on the flywheel and try to start her.

So, Charlie, with his dandy 18-foot Mullins runabout, was a real attraction for several years on the Vermilion River. The Mullins was a cute little speeder with an open cockpit, side seats for'd, a cross seat just ahead of the engine and an aft seat. The heart of the boat, in my mind, was the Roberts two-cylinder, four-cycle darling, the apple of my designs. An unusual feature of the Mullins was the underwater exhaust at the very stern which bubbled excitedly when the engine was moting.

Not only was the boat one to remember, but Charlie was a rare bird who left everlasting impressions on my boyhood memories. He was always a very old man to me with slow motion ways, a hesitant voice and a pale mellow-like face with an almost indiscernible white mustache. He was a chronic pipe smoker which took a little steadying in the jaws when first inserted in his mouth. On top of these characteristics he was a gentleman who exuded kindness to everyone. He lived in Elyria where he had been a machinist until retiring at seventy. He told me he came from New York state for a one-week visit and stayed 35 years!

On a nice day Charlie would take the New York Central "plug" to Vermilion carrying a suitcase with his "engineer" clothes. At George Goetz's he would row across the river in George's flat-bottom catboat and tow his boat back. She was moored between two stakes and covered with a snug canvas. It was a safe place to leave a boat free from dock boardings and not an open invitation for kids like us. Charlie's boat didn't have a name on her so we called her the "tin-boat" since she was all metal with pleasing lines and a popular type. Mullins of Salem, Ohio, was a leading builder of boats fabricated of press formed sheet steel; they were heavy and solid hulls with a smooth skin, designed for a lifetime of service.

If Charlie docked next to George's gill-net tug for greater privacy, I would board the tug and sit watching Charlie's every move, fascinated by the expected engine start-up and his ingrained habits from years as a machinist. He was as much fun as the engine, almost. I hung on without disturbing the engineer and he was too much of a gentleman to chase me away. What could anyone do with a sticker like me?

The first operation was to get the engineer pants on and then go through the routine of starting the motor. After dressing he took a wad of cotton waste from the tool drawer and polished the engine so she looked spick and span. Then he moved to the linoleum around the engine and gave that a good polish. These were all rituals as certain as the turning of the earth but fun for Charlie. He was a natural fiddler and his actions impressed me as you can see. I guess this is why old folks are called fuds or fuddy duddies.

Now the Roberts was a cranky engine to start sometimes and when that happened he would sit back, light his pipe and "give her a rest" as he would say, but meaning he needed the rest. At his age cranking a flywheel in the position required was a chore. All these years later I have concluded that his problem must have been due to that underwater exhaust and the water vapor that came up the pipe as the engine cooled the last time it ran. Moisture would form a water gap at the spark plug and played havoc starting. I don't think Charlie knew this little secret but it didn't cause him undue pain as the motor usually started.

The start-up followed the polishing act: he went for'd and opened the gas valve at the gas tank; then he opened the pet cocks and put a gas prime in each cylinder. Charlie then turned on the ignition switch; inserted the crank in the flywheel and gave it a fast turn over compression. If she caught-on and took-off he would sit back and catch his breath and let her run, soon shifting the throttle to varying speeds to see the response. If he was satisfied he sat down again to make doubly sure she would stay steady and keep going. When he was sure, he took the ensign from storage, unfurled it and inserted it in the aft socket; he put on his cap, adjusting it properly; refilled the pipe with a fresh charge, lighted up and puffed for a while to get it going, and cast off the lines. I assisted for I was off his boat. Now to the stern seat to try the steering wheel, get a solid bite on his pipe and push the clutch in very carefully. The tin-boat and Charlie would take off in a cloud of steam and bubbles following in his wake. I never saw his face then, but I can imagine there was a small smile on his face as he ran merrily down the river.

Charlie was a happy boater doing what he loved to do in 1920. One day a few years later when we were good friends he failed to take the tin-boat out. Charlie had passed away and his boat stayed across the river. I never did know what happened to the tin-boat, but the boat and Charlie never left my memory. They were both lovable and exotic characters to me. And you know, I never did get a chance to start that Roberts!

The Whistling Winds

Just finished reading two hurricane yarns: *Fastnet Force 10*, by John Rousmanier, and *Freshwater Fury*, by Frank Barcus, both fine descriptions of nature gone wild on salt- and freshwater. Such hurricanes as indicated should be avoided by commercial vessels, fishermen and yachtsmen with the aid of present day weather reporting technique.

I recall the early days of reporting storms on the lakes using Western Union telegrams and U.S. Mail maps that usually came after the fact, and the flags we flew generally were ignored by the fishermen. Yachtsmen were more cautious and would stay in if a Nor'wester was flown. Freighter skippers noticed the signals but shipped out on schedule regardless "'cause the storm usually never developed or amounted to no more than a strong breeze."

Those days are now over for we have an excellent weather analysis and reporting system run by the government. When they say a storm is coming, it comes. There is no more questioning the Weather Bureau, as it used to be called.

The great need for accurate reports has come from aviation and millions of people flying all over the world, not to mention shippers, fishermen and boaters. There are too many folks on the water and in the air today depending on good weather to have a faulty system. The meteorologists do a superb job.

One item in the Barcus book stopped me: he referred to "windy youngs" as a holding device on wooden hatch covers on the old freighters. Anyone know what they are and why named?

The great storm of 1913 totally destroyed 19 lake ships and stranded 20, the worst gale to hit the lakes in recorded history of the area. Two hundred and fifty one sailors lost their lives by drowning or hypothermia. That was a storm by any measure and one to remain in the memory of anyone reading *Freshwater Fury*. Barcus is also a fine pen-and-ink artist; his renderings do a better job of showing the seas than photography.

Our large vessels now on the lakes, 730 and 1000 footers, are all equipped with strong hulls, ample power to prevent "troughing" which rolled over many of the big ships in 1913, before modern electronic navigational instruments and seagoing designs to keep the sea out. The 730s have had ample proof in the oceans to test their seaworthiness in big seas. The 1000 footers are yet unproven in hurricane seas. Their baptism in maximum natural forces may never come with modern storm reporting service. Perhaps it is just as well.

The *Force 10* book is an excellent illustration of an irresponsible race committee sending thousands of yachtsmen out in a fun race in the face of bad weather reports for the English Channel in 1979. Those racing sailboats are not made to withstand the waves and forces created by 60 mile per hour gales. Some 15 sailors were lost along with 24 boats. If it hadn't been for the spectacular 'copter rescues 100 men could have met their doom in the water. Breakers 30 to 40 feet high engulfed the small hulls like toy boats. Many were rolled over completely. The 40-plus-footers managed to weather the hurricane. Some consideration to limiting hull length might be in order if weather reports are to be ignored, but I believe after that severe gale all regatta committees are going to be very careful. This is the way it should be with modern science as an ally in the fight against the whistling winds at sea.

Last of the Schooners

Upon the passing of her Aunt Lydie Wakefield in July, my daughter Mary Ann Buxton found the accompanying pictures in a desk drawer. Knowing I was the shipman who would appreciate them, she sent them to me, and I would like to share them with you.

They were photos taken by Clinton DeWitt in the summer of 1915. How these snaps happened is a story worth telling, for it goes back to the University of Michigan at Ann Arbor.

Albert Wakefield in his freshman year was pledged to Phi Kappa Sigma, a fraternity house next to Phi Delta Theta. In the course of various neighborly meetings, Al somehow found out there was another sailboater in the area, none other than Clint, a Phi Delt, hailing from Oconto, Wisconsin. He had come across the lake and deserted his University of Wisconsin to major in naval architecture that could only be had at Michigan. They became lifelong friends via their intense interest in boats, ships and sailing. Clint often visited the Wakefield house in Vermilion, now the museum.

Clint's family owned a maple floor mill in Oconto and imported maple lumber from across the lake. This afforded the opportunity the young sailors needed to hitch a passage on the lake. You can imagine the enthusiasm of sailing aboard a real live schooner by teen-agers who had sailed mere clinker knockabouts. So, the summer saw the two fans sign on the big *Alice* at Traverse City, Michigan, to Thompson, Michigan, across Lake Michigan.

On another voyage, perhaps that same summer, Clint and Al sailed aboard the *Skeele* with Captain Tom Bernstrom. This photo of the skipper shows him in typical schooner togs, all set to go to any farmer's picnic once he makes a landing. The picture taken by Clint is one of the best of a lake schooner captain at the helm; it has been published in other media and is quite well-known. Our memories of fleeting moments aboard a lake schooner have been pleasantly triggered by these 85-year-old photos. Those born by the lakes are aware of the lure.

Captain Tom Bernstrom at the helm of the Skeele. Note the size of the mizzen boom,

Schooner Alice with a deck load of maple lumber. She is close-hauled on a starboard tack in a light breeze.

Deck view looking for'd on the schooner Skeele. Al is on the left and the regular crew on the right is from the cutter Wiryinia. This is a fine deck view of a sailing lake schooner.

Ship Notes

Alice
Built in 1881 in Manitowoc, WI: Home port Milwaukee, WI.GT 307, NT 291, L 137.3, B 30.3, D 9.8, Official No. 105999.

Edward E. Skeele
Built in Milwaukee, WI, as the *Pauline*in 1856; rebuilt in 1881 as the *John Mee*, GT 199, NT 189, L 123, B 26.9, D 9; Official No. 76264; named *Edward E. Skeele*; 1920, owned by A. M. Chesbrough of Thompson, MI; 1921, owned by L. A. Buck of Escanaba, MI; Sept. 25, 1921, stranded on Barrie Island in Julia Bay on north side of Manitoulin Island, Lake Huron.

George Goetz's Fleet

George had farmed and fished off the beach at Avon Lake for some fifty years before coming to the Vermilion River in 1916. He had purchased the *Bill Murphy* land just south of the water works where he built a small house and a twine shed. His boatbuilding shed was made from the Murphy building. A large three-trunk willow tree cast a shadow over his property. He was as independent as a king secure in his castle, and no one bothered him.

He must have been near seventy when we first met, and when I left the river he was really an old man. His dress was of another era, a domed brim hat with a slightly turned down rim; heavy pants bulging at the knees, and shoes of thick leather. When he removed his hat, which wasn't often, a purple band always appeared on his forehead from the hat's grasp. It made me wince a little every time I saw the mark.

I was nine years old then and full of curiosity about fishermen, boats and engines. I watched his engine starting routines, his net making and bait cutting, and listened while he spun yarns about mammoth sturgeon he had caught off the beach at Avon, or how he used catfish grease to rub on his callused hands or leaking shoes.

"Old George" had two boats, the gas tug *Robert G.*, and the sailing rowboat without a name. The power boat was used for gill-net fishing and the sailer for trotline cat fishing. He had built both boats before I knew him. The *Robert G.* must have been named for his family or his brother's.

This little tug was about 30 feet long with a nice sheerline, a properly rounded stem and a graceful steamboat stern. She was a trim little ship much admired by boat fans. He built a box-like cabin for his pilothouse with an adjoining box to cover the engine. He had a two-cylinder, four-cycle Regal gas-kerosene engine in her, and it was fun watching him start it on gas and switch to kerosene when the motor got warmed up properly. Many times I watched the boat come to the dock with the engine running dead slow, as though George were docking a 600-foot freighter, the exhaust sounding like it was going to conk out any minute. That Regal was a fine engine. When I knew George he seldom fished gill-nets for some reason or other, perhaps because of the license cost, but I knew he had nets in storage.

The sailboat was an 18-foot, flatbottom rowboat with a centerboard amidships. George steered her with an oar in a fixed oarlock which facilitated turning, and it worked well enough for sailing to his lines a few miles west along shore. The rig was rather strange to me since the mainsail (she was cat rigged) was a normal gaff-headed sail set in reverse; that is, the leech was at the spar and the sail was supported by a split gaff that ran from the foot of the spar to the outer peak. She sailed well and made a fine catfish fisherman. When I made my first sailboat, George was the one who advised me to put a rock in the bottom for ballast, and his fixed oar idea at the stern came from his rudder. I used the normal gaff rig, though, which was the kind I knew.

I often sat and watched George overhaul his trotline in the twine shed and saw him sharpen each hook with a small stone, after which he lined each hook along the side of the box. He used stones for sinker. He had laboriously chiseled a groove in them to take the line. At other times I watched him cut bait; this consisted of slicing a large beef heart, cutting the slices into 1/2 inch cubes to entice the catfish that roamed along the beaches in the summertime. When he had a line in the lake, he would stroll out on the pier every evening with his "glasses," binoculars that were worn to the brass, to scan the west shore to see if poachers were around. He wasn't about to let any stealers take his cats. He was just as wary about his line as he was of his property. His nets, his pump and his tools were sacred and he would defend them like a tiger; as a result not many river folks were allowed to use his property unless they had been proven reliable.

I believe a brother or close relative had died and left a new Buick to George. The new possession created a storage problem, so he built a concrete block garage beside the road for the valuable new car, which he never used, leaving it to his nephew when he died. Like a squirrel, George saved everything.

When George tried to kid someone, he would elbow me a couple of times in his exuberance. He usually was the only one laughing, but that did not stop him. I always wrinkled my face pretending it was funny.

One day while passing his house, I heard loud music. One occasion he invited me in to hear the source, a player piano, a new inheritance possibly received with the Buick. The instrument was massive in the small kitchen-living room. He was tickled pink to show it off; and as he pedaled away with gusto, out came the "*Snizelbunk Polka*" loud and clear, vibrating every board in the house. He loved his latest possession.

If speeders ran their boats in the river fast enough to rock the *Robert G.*, he would shake his fist and tell them they were going too fast. He was a self-appointed harbor master, Vermilion's first. I believe he would have chastised even the Corps of Engineers if he thought they were out of line.

In those years we had several worn out two-cycle gas engine boats in the river that were hard to start. When the owner was about to give up and go home he'd try a last chance at George's dock. George loved to assist by giving advice. If he failed, he would express his final theory, "They should have put a check valve at the carburetor."
Old George was a reflection of the past, the old days in this country and Europe; he was a liv-

ing piece of history that I didn't fully appreciate at the time. But times were changing, the steam tugs were gone, the marsh was converted to lagoons and Tom Ball, Jim Brooks, Gib Snyder, Cloudy Noel, Jay Stevens, all his cronies had passed away. Then, too, a new breed of river folks were emerging —the boaters, churning the river with their plastic funboats.

Just before old George died, my brother Fred arranged to have the town buy his property for the water department expansion. Today the old man's land is the settling basin for the city waterworks.

As I look back at my river characters I have known, I realize that I was fortunate to have known George Goetz.

SC's in my Life

As a youngster growing up in the Great War, WWI, I was considerably influenced by the news and propaganda flowing from the daily papers: Massive troop losses at the fronts, sinkings at sea by the invisible submarines and the parental discussions about the war. It was an exciting growth period in our young lives. With paper sailor hats, Civil War swords and the music from Sousa's band, such popular war songs as "Over There" and "Johnny Get Your Gun" played on the new wind-up Victrola, we marched. That was heady stuff for kids. We were ready to enlist even though we were way under age. So, when Father asked me to accompany him to Rocky River to see some navy boats under construction at the Zikes' boat yard, I jumped at the chance. We took the Lake Shore Electric interurban to see the sub chasers!

At Rocky River we walked down a long stair to the lower boat yard and entered a large shed. There stood tremendous wooden hulls that loomed above us with bare planking seemingly staring at the observers. The aroma of wood permeated the building. We were impressed with the entire operation and to know that these ships would help win the war at sea. Father and I returned knowing that our trip satisfied our beliefs that the country was doing all it could to assist in fighting the under-sea boats that were sinking so many of our ships.

The war was won and the chasers did their share in convoy duty and attacking submarines. In 1924 Father built his "iron ship" and we cruised to Florida on the inside passage which in those days was pretty hectic. At Norfolk, Virginia, we lay overnight in a lagoon, the Hague, someplace in the city. Since there were no open docks we tied alongside a naval vessel. In the morning we discovered the naval vessel to be a group of sub chasers in the throes of being dismantled and scrapped. I was thrilled to be able to walk around the boats and to inspect them casually for they were my favorite war ships. Hadn't I observed their birth at Rocky River?

I peered into the engine room hatch and it was bare; the three Standard engines had been removed, nothing but the bilge water reflected the past history of the ship. It gave me a ghostly feeling tempered with the pungent odor of gas and oil. It was a dramatic exposure and I never forgot my visit to the retired sub chasers in the Hague at Norfolk. I understand the lagoon is still there but a barrier bridge isolates the place.

Subchaser SC 143 built in Rocky River, one of 450 built to fight the U-Boats in World War I. U.S. Navy photo.

The next chapter in this sub chaser yarn took place quite unexpectedly 42 years later in a small village, New Hampton, New Hampshire. There, through my daughter Alice I met a fine artist by the name of Fritz Robbins. We visited him in his 18th century house where he showed his collection of art work. In the ensuing conversation, and before we realized it, we were talking about the Navy. Fritz just happened to mention that he had been an engineer on a sub chaser in WWI! That did it, from then on the subject of art was a dead duck for he held sway and told about his experiences aboard ship. Many were related to gasoline fires in the engine room; one was when he saved his buddy by pulling him out. Well, the final result of Fritz Robbins' meeting the chaser buff from Lake Erie, was Fritz sending me an original watercolor of a chaser at sea. I still have the picture and often think of Fritz and fighting gas fires on his boat.

Now it is 1989 and last month my son-in-law. Angus Murdoch, director of the Life-Saving Museum of Virginia at Virginia Beach, wrote me an interesting letter. He stated that he had met a retired commercial fisherman from North Carolina who fished the last sub chaser hull. She had been converted, and had been lost off Nova Scotia in 1987. She was the last of the 450 chasers and when you consider her age of 70 years, those boats must have been well built. So, the sub chasers are gone but the tale goes on: Angus also referred me to two chaser books now in my hands that offer fine reading for powerboat sailors. He also proved the numbers of chasers built in Rocky River from a 1919 Jane's reference: 142, 143, 403, 404, 405, 406, 437, and 438. Were any of these ships I inspected at the Hague in 1924? I often wonder; but in those years I was too excited about being aboard to list the figures at the bow. Besides, how was I to know I would be writing a yarn for *Inland Seas* about sub chasers in 1989? The coincidence of seeing a Rocky River boat would have been a rare and good ending for this story, but it did not happen.

Here is what did happen, which is about as interesting and rare: Alexander Moffat (many yachtsmen know this chap for his cruising stories) wrote his memories in a book called *The Maverick Navy* in 1976 about his experiences on a chaser in the English Channel during WWI. His boat was SC 143, the one I saw being built at Rocky River! Thus ends my story about SCs in my life.

Introduction to the *Skeele*

In last winter's *Lure* I told you about finding brother Al's photographs of the schooner *Edward E. Skeele*, and since then another picture has come to light from his collection, a fine full view of the ship at a dock in Marinette. Then, out of the blue, the complete story of the *Skeele* was sent to me by Walter Hirthe of Milwaukee who had noticed the schooner story in the *Lure*. This was a real exposure and so interesting that I am reproducing it here for ship lovers everywhere. Walter and his wife did a thorough job in researching the history of the vessel and its untimely end. We thank the Wisconsin Marine Historical Society for permission to reprint this contribution to schooner history which appeared in their *Soundings*.

The Search for the *Skeele*

by Walter M. and Mary K. Hirthe

She was built as the schooner *Pauline* in 1856 at Milwaukee by George Barber for Philip Lawrence, Zacharias Saveland, Tonnes Saveland and Andre Olson with Z. Saveland as master. Her measurements were about 105 x 27 x 9 feet and 214 tons. The *Pauline* became property of William Johnson of Chicago before the season of 1865. He owned the schooner for over 15 years and during this period she was involved in only a few minor mishaps. The vessel was sold to William W. Chapin of Manistee in the fall of 1880 and, after only one round trip, she was struck down by the Alpena Gale, one of the great storms of the century.

In the vicinity of Baileys Harbor, the gale arrived from the northwest on Friday evening, October 15, 1880, but deceived the many vessels seeking shelter in the harbor by suddenly shifting to the southeast at about 2 a.m. Saturday. The *Pauline*, with Capt. John Anderson, was a late arrival at about 6 p.m. Saturday loaded with lumber and shingles for South Chicago. She let go her anchors but carried away her cabin and windlass at about 7 p.m. to join three schooners already resting in the sand at the north end of the harbor. The crew took to the rigging where they stayed all night and were taken off in the morning by a pound net boat.

The hull of the *Pauline* was sound but the work of getting her off was abandoned in November, late in the season. Chapin returned in June 1881 with the tug *Caroline Williams* of Manistee to reclaim the *Pauline*. After dredging a channel through the sand well up on the beach about a half mile east of the range lights, the schooner was pulled into open water and towed to the Milwaukee Shipyard Co. In the fall of 1881, she was reconstructed and renamed *John Mee*. A third mast was added consistent with the increase in length of 20 feet, and the carrying capacity was raised to 150,000 feet of lumber.

Chapin sold the *Mee* to John Thompson, Nels Olson and Louis Olson, vessel owners of *Sheboygan*, before the season of 1888. She became the *John Mee* of Chicago before the season of 1898, and the property of the Chicago Transportation Co. in spring 1911. At the end of the season, the *John Mee* was renamed *Edward E. Skeele*. This was the second alias for the *Pauline* as she continued to roam the waters of Door County.

The Skeele at the lumber slip in Marinette. A hull of fine lines not yet hogged from age, a nicely curved clipper bow with a classic stern properly slanted at the transom. The white topsides lend a suitable accent for her sheer. The rigging is clearly visible and is typical for a laker of the day complete with rafee yard at the foremast. Topsails are furled and stopped at the foot of the topmasts. Note the heights of the topmasts and their various length quite different from saltwater coasters that sported even length masts. I have heard that the lakers reached skyward with topmasts to gather the light summer zephyrs that are so prevalent on the lakes. Anchors are catted ready to drop, one of the most important pieces of equipment aboard a sailer for they usually needed them quickly. Skippers were very skilled at sailing into harbors and docks without tugs if the wind was right, but the tugs were necessary to assist in currents or contrary winds. The classic lake schooner such as the Skeele inherited much in design and construction from saltwater craftsmen because the men came from the seaboard, where the clippers were born, during the schooner building era—1840-1880.

The Skeele stranded on the rocky shore of Julia Bay. A great silhouette of a graceful ship before she dies a sunken ending. Photo: Manitowoc Marine Museum.

From 1915 to 1920 the managing and principal owner of the *Skeele* was A. M. Chesbrough, lumberman, of Thompson, Michigan. This tiny lumber port had already gained a permanent place in Great Lakes history as a point of departure for the *Rouse Simmons*, the "Christmas Tree Ship," on her fatal voyage in 1912.

The last owners of record on the *Skeele* were Lawrence A. Buck and W. L. Kennedy of Escanaba, Michigan, as of December 24, 1920. An unusual sight was witnessed on Green Bay Wednesday afternoon December 1, 1920, when the schooner, with Capt. J. Louis Larsen, sailed into Sturgeon Bay under a full spread of canvas and came to anchor off the Goodrich dock. It was very unusual to see one of these craft in commission as late as December. The last owners of the *Skeele* were Capt. Larsen and Orin W. Angwall, who borrowed the money for the purchase from Buck, but this change of ownership was not recorded. Eyewitness accounts by Angwall, mate, and Harold W. Pripps, passenger, photographer and chronicler, document the last trip and the loss of the schooner.

She left Chicago on Saturday, September 17, 1921, for Manitoulin Island, Ontario, in Canadian waters. The master was J. Louis Larsen who was known as Louis Larsen because his father, James Larsen, had the same first name. The senior Larsen had rescued the crew of the Canadian bark *Two Friends* in North Bay during the great gale of October 1880. The story of the *Two Friends* is told in the first chapter of our book, and we were fortunate to have James Larsen appear on board the *Skeele* in the last chapter. The other members of the crew were Orville "Dewey" Stephenson of Marinette; John Locklund of Menominee, an old time sailor; and Eli Muller of Green Bay, Louis Larsen's brother-in-law.

During the trip, the captain's father was building a yawl boat on deck. The *Skeele* arrived in Julia Bay on Barrie Island on Thursday afternoon. Friday and Saturday passed uneventfully except for loading 6,000 cedar posts, and a little hunting while on the shore. On Sunday morning the crew was awakened by the howling of the wind through the rigging and the creaking of the blocks as the boat pitched about. The wind had shifted to the northwest, literally pinning the *Skeele* to the shore. The crew could not take a chance on making sail in darkness with the gale howling right into the narrow bay.

At 2:30 p.m., with winds approaching 60 m.p.h., the port anchor parted with a bang. All the chain to the starboard anchor was let out but the single chain caused the vessel to swing from side to side as she pitched in the rolling seas. Suddenly the remaining anchor began to drag, and once this hook pulled out of the mud, the progress of the *Skeele* to the foaming beach was not to be denied. The captain ordered a raft to be built because the new yawl had been washed ashore. The crew struggled to shore where they went into a cedar thicket and started a roaring fire. Angwall and Stephenson walked down an old logging road to see if they could find anyone on the island. They came back in an hour with lanterns, bearing the cheery news that they had struck a sympathetic homesteader and his wife. Mr. and Mrs. Charles Eaton took the survivors in and gave them the best they had. On Monday, September 26, Mr. Eaton took Capt. J. L. Larsen and Pripps to Gore Bay where they sent telegrams reporting the loss of the *Skeele*.

The Roaring Lake

As the northeaster screams through the willows thrashing the yellow tips,
The lake is rolling her seasong from Buffalo all the way to the ships
That push out of Toledo harbor in a rhythmic shower of spray
Of muddy Lake Erie's water stirred so thoroughly the northeaster's way.

Along shore the breakers are crashing with their interminable din,
As if fighting the landside with a thunderous force from within.
And the piers that skirt the shoreline grasping with all their might,
Resist the constant, powerful, never-ending breakers with all their fight.

The fishermen who normally lay in port wheel hard against the force
That twist them and trounce their ship all along the course;
And then on nearing port, not satisfied with leaving them alone
But try their best to crash them against the pierside stone.

A boiling, rolling mass of seaside in any man's repertoire
A mad, scrambling, crazy Lake Erie all along the battling south shore;
For it is part of the lake's picture that we often see in the year
And it's the world's famous seasong that seamen are accustomed to hear.

The Cason J. Callaway, a typical Great Lake ore carrier of the 1940's prior to the 1000 foot self-unloaders. Considered a good looking ship. Photograph by Alan W. Sweigert.

One Degree West

The rhythmic cycle of the unloading rigs were slowing down—-a sure sign of clean-up in the hold. We'll be moving out soon thought the captain as he lifted the phone to call the chief.

"Mac, you getting ready to steam?"

"Yes siree, Captain, we'll be set when you ring for it," came back over the line in a confident voice that was so typical of the after end of the *James T. Beamer*.

"The weather sounds pretty brisk from the northeast—'bout thirty miles, Mac. Better put her down so we can get some sleep up to Point Betsie."

"Aye, aye, Captain, we'll fill the tanks. Let us know when you want her lightened in case the wind flattens. I don't have much confidence in those weather guys."

Captain Jones felt very much the way Mac did but his years up forward had taught him to be prepared just in case. It could blow hard in a hurry as it often did on Lake Michigan.

Soon the clop, clop, clop of steps on the metal deck signaled the arrival of the mate. He knocked and entered with the captain's permission.

"How's the hold, Mr. Springer?"

“Well, Captain, she should be all cleaned up in an hour.”

“I’ll call the tugs in thirty minutes. Better check the crew to see that all the boys are aboard. Weather may be a bit rough on the way up if the wind hauls to the north.”

“Very good, Captain, I’ll be ready aft.”

The mate left and closed the door with a snap. He tried it again to see that it was secure.

An air of embarkation was fast settling around the *Beamer*. The deckhands felt it—even the firemen who were off watch pulsed the chain reaction of departure set off by the “old man” up forward. Soon the sputtering, steam whistle came to life and echoed a command for the tugs. As lights glittered in the evening, black smoke from the tugs quickened the pace of action. The *Beamer* was clear! The clanking chatter of winding winches accented the resounding puffing of the tugs to thrill the hardiest seaman with the drama of a moving ship.

Past the lighthouse and into the open lake, Captain Jones cleared his tugs with one long and one short blast. Mac’s screw was thumping aft as the telltale vibrations matched the heartbeat of his steamer. The *Beamer* was off and out in Lake Michigan, heading up the lakes to Duluth.

In the morning the captain arose and noted the wind from the northeast was as predicted, blowing about thirty miles an hour. He checked the ship’s position in the pilothouse and went aft for breakfast with Mac.

“Well, Mac, looks like the weather guys are on the beam this time, aye?”

“You bet, Captain, but give old man wind a chance. I’ll wager we’ll get it sooner or later. I’m not going to relax until we’re past Betsie.”

“You want another eight hours, Mac?”

“Yes siree, Cap, I don’t like the feel of this late November day on Michigan.”

The captain left Mac with his last cup of coffee and contemplated the pessimism of the chief as the deck-plate joints passed under his gaze. Why not play it safe, he reasoned. My only possible hazard now is getting caught on a lee shore with a westerly. This northeaster is set and is no problem or threat. But if it were to shift and increase in velocity from the west—ah, there is my vulnerability, and he smacked his fist into his hand to demonstrate a decision.

The third mate saw the motion through the back window of the pilothouse. Oh, oh, here comes a shift of some kind, he thought. He felt like exclaiming to the wheelsman but restrained himself like a good officer. But he was not surprised when the captain entered.

“Mr. Johnson, lay a course from our present position to the west side. We’ll run up that way just in case we need a lee from a westerly.”

"Yes sir, Captain," and the mate proceeded to the chart table. He knew the old man was training him to be a future skipper; hence, he received only a general order. He also knew the skipper would review his suggestion and discuss it before the course was altered. That was why Johnson respected Captain Jones—he knew ships, men and the weather.

The new course was now nor'west which provided a gradual lee with a continuous northing. It also fixed their position at the west side with a bearing on the light at Manitowoc.

At ten the barometer dropped to a low of 29. Mr. Anderson, the second mate, took his watch and greeted the captain. Mr. Johnson reviewed the circumstances relating to the new course and the present position so the second mate would have all the facts to facilitate safe navigation through the ten to two watch. This was the way the captain ran the ship so it was all pure routine. At ten thirty the weather changed.

"Look at that shift in wind direction, Mr. Anderson. By golly, old Mac may have been right."

"Something's brewing, Captain, when the direction of the wind shifts so quickly."

"From thirty at nor'east to thirty to due west is more than a brew, Mr. Anderson. We're going to get it!"

The wind came. In an hour the sea was so rough the captain rang up half speed for Mac as the *Beamer* was hitting the waves too hard for safety. The slackened speed eased the strain and rolling considerably.

"Captain, look over there," the mate pointed to port. "Look at that haze coming in from the west."

A wall of fog was on the horizon. By now the scud from the water was pelting the pilothouse windows like hail. Visibility dropped to a hundred feet.

"Here it comes, Captain."

The bow of the *Beamer* raised as a giant wave lifted her abnormally. Down she crashed in a mist of water-torn wind.

"These are the forerunners of a terrific sea, Mate."

Both the captain and the mate hung on as the *Beamer* fell in the trough. The wheelsman clamped his hands to the wheel. The *Beamer* rolled and pitched as succeeding seas twisted her bulk mercilessly without regard for her massive 10,000 tons.

"Captain, these seas are pushing us to starboard.We're heading north now," shouted the wheelsman.

Sure enough, concluded the captain and the mate as they checked the compass reading. The wind had blown them off course as the *Beamer* rose high in the big seas.

"Ring Mac for full speed."

"Full speed, Captain," the mate repeated.

"Full speed," the mate reported after he had signaled the chief on the chadburn.

Soon Mac's extra revolutions increased, but the vibration was diffused in the rolling and buffeting of the ship. The captain and the mate watched the compass closely for a gain west, but the compass held steady north.

"Try a thirty-five degree rudder, wheelsman, and hold it," ordered the captain.

"A couple degrees only, Captain," yelled the mate.

The *Beamer* hung on fighting every last inch just to hold her course and way. She was slugging it out in a deadly contest against the wind and sea.

By now the constant drone of the gale set the sound level in the pilothouse. The wind of eighty or ninety miles an hour literally blew the water from cresting breakers and swept it in spume along the surface of the waves. The ship was rolling frightfully by as much as thirty degrees from side to side in a slow wallow. The temperature had dropped quickly with the oncoming gale and was fast coating the deckhouse and hatch covers with succeeding layers of glaze. Soon the rail and deck-lights were battered to the deck as the sweeping breakers flattened them to offer less resistance. The burning lights cast an eerie glow through their crystal encasements. Icicles grew horizontally, shaped by the constant pressure of the wailing wind.

As the ship rolled, massive seas swept the decks and cascaded clear across to fall with retarded force in the sea again. Quick scudding coamers washed the deck with jetting fountains emerging from infinite obstructions of steel.

What was happening aft was mere conjecture as visibility cut off sight to less than amidships and Mac's phone had gone dead. It must be tough aft if it is this rugged up forward, thought the captain. But Mac was still steaming. Thank God for him. If Mac stops we're a goner, and yet we'll be lucky to stay off shore even with steam.

Hours slipped by without a ghost of abatement in the wind and noise. Hunger began to gnaw at the innards of the crew. Storm fatigue slowed responses as muscles tired from continuous gripping.

The captain conferred with his mates in the pilothouse. All three were now there along with the wheelsman, locked in a casement of ice. The conference was short and to the point.

"Men, we can hang on as long as Mac can keep going and try to outlast the gale. We may be driven ashore because our position is unknown. If we go ashore chances are we'll all perish in the ice water and surf. Any suggestions?"

"Hang on, Captain," piped the first mate.

"If we could only run with it, it would be nothing," reasoned the second mate.

"How 'bout dropping both anchors and drifting until they hold, Captain?"

"May be too deep here. A drift would be apt to capsize her with this sea."

The captain hesitated while weighing the suggestions. The last one by the third mate caused him some consternation as he could be in a suitable anchoring depth now. It also was novel enough to have some consideration.

He caught his balance between lurches and smacked his palm with a crack heard above the storm. He had made his decision.

"We'll hang on and pray for Mac."

All night long the five spent a silent vigil in the pilothouse. At daybreak mountainous seas greeted the seamen to further depress their beaten spirits. They were hanging on—but just.

"The next hour will render a verdict, men," the captain said as his words broke the suspense of the ambient tension but it unmoved the men. They knew a limited time lay ahead which might spell their doom, but they did not react. They had been brainwashed by the storm.

Mr. Johnson was at the wheel when he reported, "Captain, we gained a degree west."

"At last! We've made it!" shouted the captain.

The captain's enthusiasm broke the spell of defeat. Even the wheelsman who was sleeping on the floor caught the air of jubilance created by the one lone degree.

In another fifteen minutes the *Beamer* was heading west. She had hung on and survived!

In the lee of the Wisconsin shoreline the captain gingerly picked his way aft over the ice-glazed deck. He found the door to the galley caved in by the breakers. The room had been washed clear of stove, furniture, refrigerator and food. It had all been smashed around into a gigantic stew with broken china and knives and forks for good measure.

Down below he found Mac cleaning up.

"What the devil did you hit up for'd yesterday, Captain?"

"They were three giant waves that the wind puffed up when it hit the lake."

"I thought you were going over the top of the islands, Captain."

"They were big ones, Mac, bigger than I have ever seen."

"Hell, Captain, they must have been for I've never had breakers in my engine room before."

"I'm glad we didn't take those weather guys too seriously, aye, Mac?"

"You're right, Captain, yes siree!"

Index

M

N